WHAT OTHERS ARE SAYING ABOUT *LOVE BOLDLY*

What happens when, in a moment, the hopes and dreams you've had for your child's life seem suddenly to shatter? Becky Mackintosh writes movingly, with candor and authenticity, about how one family's journey of understanding—"refusing to take a side"—leads to life-changing enlightenment about the love our Savior and Heavenly Parents have for each one of us.

Like all chronicles shared in real-time, the Mackintoshes' story is still unfolding, and yet what is clear is that their decision to love without qualification has allowed greater compassion, empathy, and even joy. The pure love of Christ, the gift of charity, is manifest not only in family unity, but also in their deepened commitment to His gospel and church. The most challenging learning experiences include missteps: Becky generously shares even those moments that in retrospect she wishes she could change, words she would want to take back, well-intended prescriptions she would later understand as shallow and hurtful. She allows us to learn through her family's transformative experiences.

Love Boldly will provide each reader an opportunity to reflect on our individual commitment as a follower of Jesus Christ, to ponder whether our own efforts on behalf of "the least of these," whoever we conceive them to be, would allow observers to identify us in His challenging commandment: "By this shall all men know that ye are my disciples, if ye have love one to another."

—Tom Christofferson, author of
*That We May Be One: A Gay Mormon's
Perspective on Faith and Family*

This book is such a gift to the world. So often we talk about the "what," sometimes the "why," but rarely do we get a peek into the "how." Becky shares the how. How to love and to wrestle in the paradoxes.

—Ganel-Lyn Condie
Speaker and best-selling author

So many LDS parents ask for a book recommendation when their kids come out as gay. *Love Boldly* is that book. It validates every emotional step along the journey from fear to love, helping parents understand themselves as well as their children. Becky Mackintosh nails it for parents who don't want to choose between their religion and their child.

—Lisa Tensmeyer Hansen, PhD, LMFT
Flourish Counseling Services, PLLC

Love
BOLDLY

Love BOLDLY

EMBRACING YOUR LGBTQ
LOVED ONES *and* YOUR FAITH

by
Becky Mackintosh

CFI
AN IMPRINT OF CEDAR FORT, INC.
SPRINGVILLE, UTAH

This is not an official publication of The Church of Jesus Christ of Latter-day Saints. The opinions and views expressed herein belong solely to the author and do not necessarily represent the opinions or views of Cedar Fort, Inc. Permission for the use of sources, graphics, and photos is also solely the responsibility of the author.

ISBN 13: 978-1-4621-3594-3

Published by CFI, an imprint of Cedar Fort, Inc.
2373 W. 700 S., Springville, UT, 84663
Distributed by Cedar Fort, Inc., www.cedarfort.com

Library of Congress Control Number: 2019946205

Cover design by Shawnda T. Craig
Cover design © 2019 Cedar Fort, Inc.
Edited and typeset by Heather Holm

Printed in the United States of America

10 9 8 7 6 5 4 3 2 1

Printed on acid-free paper

CONTENTS

PROLOGUE

By Sean Mackintosh

I thought I'd take my secret to the grave. In fact, I preferred to die rather than have anyone else find out. And I almost did die, several times, by my own hand.

I was raised in a typical Latter-day Saint family—large and orthodox. We attended Sunday meetings and held Monday family home evenings together. We said our nightly prayers and studied the scriptures daily. We did everything that good Latter-day Saint families do to ensure that they will be a forever family. I loved my family and certainly wanted to be with them forever. I strived to be obedient to the commandments—all of them—as best I could. I received my Duty to God Award, held numerous Church callings, graduated from seminary, and served an honorable mission. Through it all, I kept a secret I feared could destroy everything I worked for. I hoped it would never get out, that it would somehow go away. But the harder I prayed, the more aware I became that neither would be the case.

In elementary school, I was like the other kids. Well, except for one gargantuan difference. While my friends were noticing cute girls and talking about their crushes on them, I was noticing the cute boys and not breathing a hint of my crushes on them to another soul. This wasn't something I had seen or heard anything about. I didn't even know what the word "gay" meant, or what a gay person was. But I remember, all too well, that I realized at a very young age I was somehow different from everyone else I knew. And I didn't think it was a good kind of different. Sometimes I became convinced that I was bad, deep down inside, so I had to make sure nobody saw the "real me." I felt ashamed of who I thought the real me was.

As I aged and the weight of my secret grew, I began to watch everything I did—how I walked, talked, and looked at other guys (while trying not to look at other guys). I was careful in choosing friends, the music I listened to, and the interests and hobbies I pursued. Nobody sat me down and told me these rules. I'd gleaned them from society, from church, and even from my family. As I spent more and more time trying to be who I thought I should be, I became less and less able to just be myself.

This was so exhausting and depressing. But, of course, I couldn't let anyone know how depressed I was, because then they'd want to know why I was depressed in the first place. So not only did I hide who I was, but I also hid how I felt and how I struggled to stay afloat. I put a smile on my face and held onto hope. I constantly pleaded and prayed with God, begging Him to take my attractions away. Yet, I remained the same, only more disheartened.

I remember I was thirteen years old when I first had the idea of killing myself. I felt so alone and isolated. I couldn't even feel my family's love, because I felt that if they knew the real me, they wouldn't love me anymore. I was sure nobody could love the real me. Not even God could love the real me.

I was only thirteen years old! Thinking that death might be my only escape continued through my teen years. I am so thankful and feel lucky to be alive today. So many kids in my same situation have not been so fortunate.

By the time I was old enough to go on a mission, I started hoping that one of the blessings of my missionary service would be that my attractions to other guys would go away. I felt I was showing God how much I loved Him and wanted to serve Him so He would finally reward me for all my days, months, and years of fasting, prayer, and service. But after returning home from serving a faithful mission, it quickly became apparent that God had a different plan for me. I was crushed to discover that, in addition to my attractions, my secret became even more difficult to keep. As a returned missionary, I was constantly being asked who I was dating. Why wasn't I dating? Didn't I know it was time for me to get married?

I started making up lies to cover the truth. I so desperately wished I could marry a woman, but that seemed impossible, because I wasn't physically attracted to them. Nor did I feel the type of emotional bond that's needed to pursue and sustain a relationship/partnership over time. It became too mentally and spiritually exhausting to keep trying.

Finally, one night I was at my wits' end. As I prayed, I felt an impression—an impression that didn't make sense at the time. I felt that instead of asking God to change me for the millionth time, I should ask for something different. I asked God how He felt about me and if He loved me for who I was rather than for what I was trying to be. It was the first time in my life I dared to ask God if it was okay for me to be me.

I had never felt the spirit stronger than I did that night. And I hadn't realized just how severely depressed I had been until I felt such complete love and joy. God loved me, and I knew He loved me!

Next, I needed to learn how to love myself and trust that others loved me too. At age twenty-four, although I was petrified, I finally came out to my parents. It didn't go well, but at least it was better than how I feared it might go. Soon after coming out to my parents, I came out to my siblings. Some were supportive, and others were disappointed—even critical. Because they didn't understand, they thought it was something I had chosen or wasn't working hard enough to overcome.

Through the many tears that followed, I would call to mind (and heart) the love I felt when God let me know that He loves me for me. Regardless of how anyone else felt, I knew my Heavenly Father loved me and that's what mattered most.

I was feeling love for the first time. I was still that son and brother they had always loved. I was still a good person who was willing to help anyone. Except now, I was being me. The real me. I wasn't lying, hiding, or feeling shameful. I wasn't worried about how I walked or talked. I wasn't embarrassed about liking Taylor Swift. I was loved for who I was. I was feeling real love.

And now? I am so grateful I did not take my life at the age of thirteen, fourteen, fifteen, or twenty-four. I have a great life, and I have been together with an incredible guy for a few years now. We purchased our first home last year and are building a wonderful life together. He has a family that loves and welcomes me, just as my family loves and supports him. I don't say this to imply that things are perfect or that it has not been a difficult process along the way.

My parents and I have mutual love and respect for one another. I am grateful that they embrace me and that they embrace their faith too. I respect their agency just as they respect mine.

I realize that not everyone will be happy with my life. However, I am. I know that my family loves me. I know that my Heavenly Father loves me and has a plan for me. And really, that's what counts the most.

AN INTRODUCTION

Once upon a time, an old farmer, who had worked his crops for many years, lost his horse when it ran away. Upon hearing the news, his neighbors came to visit. "Such bad luck," they said sympathetically.

"Maybe," the farmer replied.

The next morning the horse returned, bringing with it three other wild horses. "How wonderful," the neighbors exclaimed.

"Maybe," replied the old man.

The following day, his son tried to ride one of the untamed horses, was thrown, and broke his leg. The neighbors again came to offer their sympathy on his misfortune.

"Maybe," answered the farmer.

The day after, military officials came to the village to draft young men into the army. Seeing that the son's leg was broken, they passed him by. The neighbors congratulated the farmer on how well things had turned out.

"Maybe," said the farmer.[1]

—*A Taoist Tale*

I have learned so many important lessons since our son Sean first messaged us to say, "Mom, Dad, I'm gay." This ever-changing journey has not been all bad or all good—as with most things in

---

1. Author unknown. See emptygatezen.com/teaching/2017/4/7/story-of-the -old-farmer; accessed July 16, 2019.

life. I've gained a great deal of empathy and compassion, especially when I meet active Latter-day Saint parents who feel that such a declaration is the worst thing they could ever hear one of their children say.

It's true that when it comes to same-sex attractions and the gospel of Jesus Christ, there is often deep pain, conflict, and grief, not to mention resentment toward God and His gospel and a sense of failure as a parent. The list of different reactions is long. I am grateful that the Savior's love is infinite.

Sometimes parents feel they need to choose a side. They think they must either reject the gospel while loving their child or hold strong to the faith while rejecting their child. However, there are far more options than these. My hope is that together we can find ways for families to remain close while living true to their beliefs, however each person might define them.

In this book, I discuss how refusing the temptation to take sides applies to my gay son, the rest of our family, and the gospel of Jesus Christ. Much of what I have learned since Sean came out to us also applies to anyone whose journey has currently taken them away from The Church of Jesus Christ of Latter-day Saints for totally different reasons.

An article written by Chelsea Homer offers valuable insights that can be applied universally. Her husband's beliefs changed shortly after they were married.

> Faith and religious activity are personal, and as such, they don't always follow the same trajectory as that of a spouse, friend, or neighbor. [Or a child, I would add.] The last few years have given me a front-row seat into the lives of many who, like us, are fighting to stay in the Church. If you can't see it, I encourage you to move in. Move in to see the young man who no longer wants to serve a mission but is too terrified to tell his leaders and peers. Move in to see the mother hurting because her children are ostracized in Primary. Move in to see the LGBTQ youth who are trying to reconcile their personal feelings in the context of the gospel of Jesus Christ. Move

in to see what an amazing man my husband is, regardless of where he is in his faith. There are so many people in need of love.[2]

I am deeply grateful that my husband, Scott, and I have reached a place with our son where he knows that we love him regardless of, and because of, our religious beliefs. We have welcomed the young men he has dated into our home, just as we have welcomed the dates, and spouses, of our other children. Some people might think that we are condoning sin. We think it's being Christlike.

This experience has strengthened my faith and my love for our son and the rest of our family. My story is included on the Church's Mormon and Gay website. There I state the following:

> I am a Latter-day Saint and I have a gay son. I love him with all my heart, might, and soul. And I love my religion with all my heart, might, and soul. It's the core of who I am. I will never, never ever turn my back on my son, and I will never, never ever leave my religious faith. Period. I've been asked how and why. It's because God has made it clear to me that I am to love my son Sean unconditionally. I admit it took me awhile to truly understand what "unconditional love" meant, because at first I confused "loving" with "condoning."

Unfortunately, but understandably, some parents feel that letting a same-sex partner participate in family activities is wrong and sets a bad example. I bear witness that the best example we can show our kids is to follow the Great Exemplar. The Savior asks us to open our hearts in hope, faith, and charity toward all of His children—especially those we parent—whether our children are "active" in the Church or not. Cutting off love does

---

2. Chelsea Homer, "Who Do I Choose—God or My Husband?" See churchofje-suschrist.org/blog/who-do-i-choosegod-or-my-husband?lang=eng, July 25, 2018; accessed July 11, 2019.

not endear anyone toward the source of such harshness, nor that which anyone might claim as a belief system.

An excellent example of how to treat children who come out as gay or who reveal that they are attracted to the same sex comes from Tom Christofferson, the brother of Elder D. Todd Christofferson. In his book entitled *That They May Be One*, Tom talks about the power of his parents' unconditional love. When Tom brought his male partner home to visit, his parents made a point of showing love to both of them. They also welcomed them at family gatherings.

Tom's story is important, because it shows the beauty and majesty of charity—the pure love of Christ. He says,

> In my view, we are unlikely in this life to ever fully have all the answers we seek, but we always know the first and second great commandments (see Matthew 22:36–40). And when we understand that "charity is the pure love of Christ" (Moroni 7:47), we find both purpose and incentive to let go of ideas that being gay is a lack of faith or an unwillingness to do hard work, that parents are at fault if children are gay, or that persons with such attractions are enemies of God.[3]

Tom's parents exhibited the Christ-centered charity back during a time when few people even in the secular world were accepting or understanding. They have illustrated the good that can come of it, with one son becoming an Apostle and their other sons becoming good men too. Tom credits the love he felt from his family and the prayers offered in his behalf for helping him experience a change of heart, get rebaptized, and return to full fellowship. He also cautions wisely that his mortal journey is not the same as anyone else's journey. Nor is it over yet.

---

3. Tom Christofferson, *That We May Be One* (Salt Lake City: Deseret Book, 2017), n.p.

Being gay is something many Latter-day Saints feel the need to keep secret, often harboring great shame for having such feelings in the first place. That shame is of the adversary, not the Lord. We know people do not choose to be gay. This is repeated by Church leaders and others on the Mormon and Gay website, as well as in conference addresses.

Regardless of the causes, shame diminishes our feelings of the spirit. It works against our spiritual and emotional health. Some parents feel great shame upon hearing one of their children is gay, as if they are somehow at fault. It is nobody's "fault." It is part of the mortal experience that includes many stalwart Saints.

Some parents of LGBTQ individuals feel they are the last to learn that their child is gay and/or attracted to the same sex. Other parents might learn secondhand or stumble upon such knowledge in another way. It is often so scary for youth to open up, especially to their parents. Although it isn't easy, I have learned how important it is to be as kind and as understanding as possible. People often know little about this topic. However, we do know about the gospel of Jesus Christ. We cannot control how or when we find out about our child's sexual orientation or attractions, yet moving forward, we *can* control how we respond. We can seek gratitude and love and trust in the Lord's timing. We can learn and grow together.

My son waited to come out to us until he was twenty-four years old. That seemed like an awful long time for him to keep such a secret, all the while fearing rejection. For years, he endured living with that secret, needlessly suffering in silence and shame.

I've spoken with many wonderful people who have had their coming out letter written and ready to give to their parents for several years. They were waiting for the right time and place, with fear often standing in the way. Some didn't tell a soul until they were in their thirties or forties. I even met a man who didn't tell anyone until he was seventy-two. No one should have to suffer so long in silence.

I have also learned how important it is for parents and children to be as understanding and patient with each other as possible. This can be a frightfully new process, which often takes time to adjust to for all those involved. It is new territory, but it doesn't have to be the final territory. Your new path together will be different than either of you had imagined. But with the Savior's love and help, it doesn't have to be lonely. You don't have to choose between your child and your faith. You can embrace both.

I have discovered something else in all of this. I have never met a Latter-day Saint LGBTQ child who said they decided to become active in the gospel again, or remain active, because their parents had rejected them. Where rejection *has* occurred, those LGBTQ who do return say they did so *in spite of* the rejection—against all odds.

How can we respond if our child says, "Mom, Dad, I am gay"? In the following chapters, I'll share what I've learned and experienced while our family has traveled this road of uncertainty—our ups and downs, mistakes, and triumphs. Because our son came out on a video, I have had the opportunity to meet hundreds of parents and LGBTQ individuals from all around the world who are navigating similar journeys. Their stories have deeply touched me and challenged me in ways I never thought possible.

Because of how much I have learned so far, and how many families I have met who are seeking understanding, I decided it was important for me to write this book.

I have continually prayed for help from above, because I have felt so inadequate. I'm not a professional therapist. I'm not a professional writer. I am a mother who dearly loves her children and the gospel of Jesus Christ. My husband, Scott, and I have served in countless Church callings to the best of our ability. Scott is currently the bishop of a young adult ward and has put into practice much of what we have learned together as parents of a gay son and six other grown children who are not gay.

I hope this book will help others walk a similar journey. Although every story is different, I hope people will feel less lonely and more companionship from the Holy Spirit and from those of us who seek to live worthy of that Spirit. Holding fast to the iron rod can bring inspiration and new ideas to help with each unique journey. Traveling this journey together is much better and easier than trying to travel it alone.

As an Important Aside . . .

There are no universally accepted terms when it comes to lesbian, gay, bisexual (LGB), and those who are attracted to the same sex but may not identify as L, G, or B. They might use the descriptor of same-sex attraction, same-gender attraction, or SSA. When speaking to an individual attracted to the same sex, there's nothing wrong with asking how they prefer to identify themselves. In fact, it can help show that you understand how complicated all of this can be and, in some ways, how simple.

In this book, I use the descriptor of gay or LGBTQ for simplicity's sake. It encompasses the spectrum of lesbian, gay, bisexual, and more. It also refers to transgender, queer, or questioning. The acronyms are in flux and can differ depending on personal preference. Some people add a + after the Q, or the letters I and A, which stand for intersex and asexual. Transgender and intersex refer to gender, not to sexual attractions or sexual orientation. And, if you're thinking it's all too confusing to bother with, I would ask that you remember that it may matter very much to your child, your friend's child, or a child of God. Because it is important to my son and many people I have met, it has become important to me.

I recognize that my experience as the mother of a gay child is very different from that of a parent raising a transgender child, which can be even more challenging to navigate. As Church leaders have stated on the Mormon and Gay website:

> Many of the general principles shared on this website (for example, the importance of inclusion and kindness) apply to Latter-day Saints who experience gender dysphoria or identify as transgender. However, same-sex attraction and gender dysphoria are very different. For example, those who experience gender dysphoria may or may not also experience same-sex attraction, and the majority of those who experience same-sex attraction do not desire to change their gender. From a psychological and ministerial perspective, the two are different.[4]

Also, if a person identifies as lesbian, gay, or bisexual, that doesn't necessarily mean that they're sexually active. They are saying that they're attracted to people of the same sex (lesbian or gay) or both sexes (bisexual). The Church of Jesus Christ of Latter-day Saints takes a stance regarding actions, *not* attractions, orientation, or identity.

---

4. The Church of Jesus Christ of Latter-day Saints, "Frequently Asked Questions: Why Does the Website Not Discuss Gender Dysphoria or Transgender Issues?" See mormonandgay.lds.org/articles/frequently-asked-questions; accessed July 11, 2019.

Chapter One

"MOM, DAD, I'M GAY."

And whoso receiveth you, there I will be also, for I will go before your face. I will be on your right hand and on your left, and my Spirit shall be in your hearts, and mine angels round about you, to bear you up.

—D&C 84:88

"Mom, Dad, I'm gay." That declaration from our son hit me like a ton of bricks hurled through a window—the window I had gazed through so many times while envisioning my son's future: a temple marriage, raising a family of his own, and the daughter-in-law and grandchildren I would adore. All of that was shattered to pieces that night in January 2012 when I read the private Facebook message from Sean:

> Hey, so I'm not gonna beat around the bush too much. I'm just going to tell you something that I'm sure you already know, or that has crossed your mind. Mom, Dad—I'm gay. I'm sure this isn't the

best news a parent could hear, but I feel it's not right for me to avoid telling you about something very real to me. I'm still very much your same weird son. Ha! I love you and dad so much, and you're the best parents a kid could ask for. That is why it's taken me so long to tell you. I'm fine with the pain it can bring me, but I just didn't want to hurt you, cause you don't deserve it. I'm keeping this brief, cause I'm sure you'd rather talk in person, and I am totally fine with that. I wanted you and dad to be the first to know. I haven't told anyone—ever.

As I stared at my computer screen and gasped for air, a flood of emotions hit me. My eyes welled up with tears. The shock of reading "I'm gay" was somewhat alleviated when I read Sean's last sentence about how he hadn't told anyone else yet. I was relieved, because I figured that if no one else knew, maybe there was still time to help "fix" what I saw as a problem before anyone else had to find out. I certainly did not want anyone else to find out such a "horrible" thing about my son. I started to hyperventilate. I couldn't think of anything worse than having a gay son. I had to fix this. Certainly God would guide me in how to fix this. He would not send this challenge to my son without a solution.

Sean was right. The idea of him being gay had crossed my mind. Sure, it had crossed my mind. I'd wondered many times why my genuinely kind, spiritually devoted, and strikingly handsome son only dated girls when they took the initiative to ask him out. He never seemed interested in being more than friends with any of them.

He just doesn't want to have a girlfriend before his mission, I'd say to myself while trying to ignore what I really thought. Now Sean had given it form, right there in black and white. I was shocked and not the least bit surprised, both at the same time.

His father, on the other hand, had no clue. He was completely blindsided by the news. It shook him to the very core. After reading Sean's message, he stormed into our room to talk to me about it. Obviously, Sean had been wise in giving us time to react without him there. Scott and I have long since been grateful for that.

I called Sean and asked him to hurry home. It was definitely not something I wanted to discuss on the phone. I wanted to see my son face to face. I wanted to hold him and be with him. I wanted to feel that he was the same son I'd loved, nurtured, and raised; the same son he was before I read his earth-shattering news.

But how could I be the same mother? So many feelings overwhelmed me as I tried to think of what I should say to him. I knew how crucial our reaction would be for him. I knew he wanted to feel our abiding love, not my sheer panic.

I fell to my knees and pleaded with God. "Please take this away. Help me know what I'm supposed to say and do. How can we make this all better? Surely it's just a phase. Did I do something wrong to make him feel this way?"

I felt I had let God down in my role as a Latter-day Saint parent given the sacred stewardship to raise my children in righteousness. What did we do that was so wrong as his parents who held such a sacred stewardship?

My angst and numbness from the shock of it all made it difficult to think straight and discern anything. Sean got home late, so I had plenty of time to try to sort things through. Mostly I had to try to regain my composure. I was a mess, and I didn't want Sean to see that.

Scott tried to wait up with me, but the late hour was too much for him, and he eventually dozed off. I was okay with him falling asleep, because I knew he was angry, and I wasn't certain how he would respond when Sean walked through the door.

I continued to wait.

And wait.

After what seemed like an eternity, Sean finally returned home. He looked scared and disheveled. He'd been dreading to have the talk that night. He'd been dreading that talk most of his life. He hoped for kindness while fearing rejection.

As my six-two, lanky son of twenty-four years stood in front of me, it seemed as if everything had suddenly changed. We sat down on the couch together. I didn't know what to say. We'd always had a good relationship, but we were both so uncomfortable.

Fortunately, I sensed that it was important for me to listen—really listen—while trying hard not to look as shocked and distressed as I felt. So I *did* listen. I tried to make sense of what I was hearing. Each sentence was as difficult as the next for both of us. I felt his pain and deep sorrow in a way that only a mother can feel. I can't remember much of what he actually said, but I do remember the anguish we both felt—for completely different reasons, yet for the same reason.

When Sean finished talking about his attractions for other guys, his feelings about the gospel, and how much all of it had affected his life, I held him close. I told him how much I loved him and that my love would never change. That was the one thing I was sure of, and I wanted Sean to be sure of my deep and abiding love for him.

I wish I could have left it at that for our first talk. (Hindsight brings such wisdom.) Instead, I told Sean what I thought he should do, as if I knew what he'd been going through or anything about what it's like to be gay and a Latter-day Saint. It was like I'd forgotten all those years my son faithfully attended Primary, Sunday School, sacrament meeting, seminary, Young Men, and served a mission. I spoke what I thought would be words of comfort and hope. Instead, I was unintentionally shooting dagger after dagger into my dear son's heart.

He listened patiently. At some point, I finally realized that the more I said the more Sean was sinking down into the couch. His spirit was sinking too. My best intentions, those things I said in a genuinely caring way that I thought would be so helpful, were actually making him feel worse. Upon realizing my mistake, I dropped the preaching and had a real soul-to-soul conversation with him.

I breathed in the spirit and slowly exhaled my angst-ridden, hyper-alert posture. I called to heart my mantle as his mother and recognized that he was the same kid I'd always known and loved so dearly. As we spoke, Sean felt safe to tell me about the many years he'd contemplated ending his life so no one would ever have to know that he was gay. I felt a deep sense of gratitude as I placed my hand on his leg—both as a gesture of love and to make sure my son was still there. He was still alive. I would later learn that many LGBTQ youth struggle with suicidal thoughts. My heart weeps for those families who have lost a child or loved one in that way.

Sean opened up about all the fear he had surrounding his sexual orientation—the fears of rejection, of hurting his family, that he wouldn't be loved anymore, that he'd be treated differently, that God would be angry with him, and that coming out would negatively impact his relationships with family and friends.

He had also grown weary of pretending to be someone he wasn't. He hated the frequent questions such as "Who are you dating?" and "Why aren't you dating?" He was nervous about coming out while attending a Church school. He'd felt those fears countless times until he reached the point where they seemed worse than staying silent and worse than staying shut down on who he really was. Admitting it to himself had been terrifying enough. He finally reached the point where the pain and isolation of staying silent seemed worse than facing his fear of rejection and condemnation.

We talked until 4:00 a.m. I hugged him tight and told him how much I loved him. As I crawled into bed, Scott awoke and asked where I had been. I told him I had been down talking to Sean and gave him the condensed version of our conversation. He immediately got up and headed toward the door. I said, "Please be kind." I wasn't certain how Scott would respond to our son—I hoped in love and kindness—but I really didn't know what to expect, because I had seen his initial reaction to reading Sean's text. When Scott returned, he said, "I just opened my arms, gave him a big hug, and told him I loved him. I told him we would talk about it later." I was so proud of Scott. I hugged him and said, "We'll figure this out."

Sean said it was a huge relief that his father and I finally knew. He was glad he could be honest with us and that we were responding in love (not counting the advice I'd tried to sell him on). He asked Scott and me not to tell anyone else, including his siblings. He was still in the beginning of his process of coming out and didn't want to feel any more vulnerable than he already did. He still didn't want to tell friends either, because the risk still seemed to outweigh the possible reward.

I understood Sean's fears of others finding out. For my own reasons, I felt my own fears of others finding out. I was relieved that no one else would find out—yet.

The next morning, I drove Sean to the airport so he could return to school at BYU–Hawaii. One of the hardest things I've ever done was to hug Sean goodbye that day. I knew I was sending him back out into the world where no one else knew what he was dealing with. There was so much raw emotion harboring inside me that I just wanted to run and hide until the world felt safe again.

In just a few short hours, I went from being grateful that no one else knew to being sad that no one else knew. I hated the idea of my son navigating such a challenging journey with no one by his side. He had no one to talk to about what he had just experienced—coming out to his parents. I regret that I was so caught up in my fears and worries that I didn't think about how scared and fearful he also must be.

I hugged him tight, knowing that hug would have to last for an entire year until I saw him again. I didn't want to let go. I knew it would be difficult to navigate new and unfamiliar territory, along with the myriad emotions that were being unearthed. I felt guilt and sorrow that Sean had gone through his struggles alone for twenty-four years. I felt a lot of fear for so many reasons, but mostly for how this would all play out here on earth and in the eternities. I was at a loss for words and where to turn for understanding and answers.

It wasn't long after Sean returned to school that I realized how heavy this weighed on my heart, and that I needed someone besides my husband to talk to about our situation; someone I could open up to who wasn't so emotionally involved. I asked Sean for permission to tell two people: our stake president and a close friend who'd had a son come out as gay just a few years earlier. Sean trusted my judgment and knew I'd need someone to talk to. There was Scott, but he was reacting even more like a deer caught in the headlights than I was.

Our stake president is a dear friend and former bishop for whom Scott had served as a first counselor. He'd been Sean's bishop through the latter part of his teenage years, sent him off for his mission, and was the stake president who released him after he completed the mission. Hoping to find some peace and perhaps a few answers, Scott and I met with the stake president. I appreciated how he expressed his deep love for Sean and our family. He reminded us of what a good young man Sean is and expressed his sincere love for him and our entire family. He listened, counseled by the spirit, and recommended a few resources we could find on the Church's website.

Talking with my friend Laurie, who had a son come out years earlier, was helpful for both of us. We were able to share many similar feelings and doubts. She didn't sugarcoat anything as she spoke of the challenges. She also testified of the Savior, His love, and His tender mercy toward all of us.

Scott and I also went to the temple together that first week after Sean returned to BYU–Hawaii. The temple has always been my personal place of refuge away from the hustle, bustle, and unrest of the outside world. It's where I go to find safety and freedom from the busyness. In the temple, I'm reminded of the beautiful plan of salvation and the love our Heavenly Parents have for each of their children.

Unfortunately, that trip to the temple did not provide the typical refuge. As I contemplated the plan of salvation with our new family dynamics, I felt a deep, strangely hollow pain. I fervently prayed for comfort and understanding. I wanted to know what the future held for Sean and what effect it would have on our eternal family.

I have always appreciated the opportunity to spend time in the celestial room praying and pondering the welfare of our children, especially considering the different challenges they were having. During those times, I would meditate and do my best to interpret thoughts and impressions.

This day in the temple was no different in that regard. I prayed and I listened, and I prayed some more. Soon the answer did come. Not in a whisper, nor in the wind, nor in an earthquake or fire. Rather, it came in a still, small voice. (See 1 Kings 19.) It was strong and clear, as if to leave no question of its validity and power for good:

"Love. Love Sean unconditionally."

"Love?" I questioned the Spirit.

The answer almost seemed too simple. Regardless, it was unmistakable.

"Just love my son? That I can do."

Some might think that is too simple of an answer. I wondered myself. It was simple, but challenging nonetheless. But the gospel is beautiful in its simplicity: Love God, love one another, and love ourselves. We are the ones who make things more complicated, not God. And for some reason, it is daunting to know what to do for a loved one who is gay, but it doesn't need to be. I felt a rush of the Spirit and a sense of confidence in the Lord. I leaned against my husband, and with a still, reverent voice, I shared with him my impression. Scott said he had received the same impression.

I'm so grateful for the second witness. Even though Scott and I had such different initial reactions to Sean's private Facebook message, we felt as one there in the temple that day. The Spirit increased our capacity for love—love for each other and for each member or our family.

We'd need all the faith, hope, and charity we could muster to press forward into the unknown.

Chapter Two

SEEKING DIVINE PERSPECTIVE IN AN EARTHLY REALM

If thou shalt [seek], thou shalt receive revelation upon revelation, knowledge upon knowledge, that thou mayest know the mysteries and peaceable things—that which bringeth joy, that which bringeth life eternal.

—D&C 42:61

It was Sean's eighth birthday. He and his young friends were gathered round the kitchen table, their pointy party hats pointing in all different directions. They burst into the happy birthday song as I brought in the cake topped with eight burning candles. Anticipation lit up the kids' faces. Some scooted forward and took a deep breath, holding it to be ready in case Sean missed a candle or two. Shouts were also heard from the peanut gallery:

"Take a big breath!"

"Make a wish!"

"Hurry before the candles go out!"

Sean sat there, frozen in place for a moment as he thought about what he wanted to wish for. Life had been changing for him. He'd begun to realize he was different from other boys. They talked about crushes on girls while he was starting to notice crushes on boys. He already knew what gay meant, because kids at school had been talking about it. He'd heard plenty of jokes and mean comments about gays. He stayed quiet, hoping his friends wouldn't notice his reluctance to join in.

So, on his eighth birthday, instead of wishing for a dinosaur or a majestic white swan like he'd done in previous years, Sean made a wish of a different sort altogether. He made an urgent plea to his Father in Heaven: "Please God, don't let me be gay. Please, I don't want to be gay." Sean blew out all eight candles at once, expelling the breath he'd been holding for so long. He made that same wish on many birthdays, and so many other days that followed.

I cried when Sean finally told me about his eighth birthday—some sixteen years later. My heart broke as I thought of my little boy pleading with God to take away his attractions to other boys. And my heart broke, because he went twenty-four years without telling another soul.

At first I couldn't understand how he could think he was gay at such a young age. Then I remembered my first crush: little Johnny Carson. (No, not the talk show host.) Johnny was in my first-grade class in Dillon, Montana. No one could have convinced me that my feelings for him weren't real. I even drew pictures of us holding hands, with a heart above our heads. Although I never actually held his hand, I knew I liked him. And if I knew I liked boys as young as first grade, it made sense that Sean could feel that way too.

I believed him, and I also believed in miracles. So, I became the one who started praying, "Please God, don't let my son be gay."

I asked Sean not to tell anyone at BYU–Hawaii that he was gay until after he'd graduated. I didn't want him to get kicked out of college. He lovingly said, "Mom, it's not against the honor code to be gay. It's against the honor code to break the law of chastity. I haven't done anything to break the honor code. I've never kissed a guy or held a guy's hand."

When I asked about girls, he said, "I've kissed girls and held their hands, so I *know* I'm not attracted to them. I've tried, Mom. Believe me, I have tried."

He added, "People don't just choose to be gay. Why would I choose something that causes such conflict? I didn't choose to be gay."

I hugged him tight as I slowly felt my heart expand and the shell around my mind peel away as it let go of false beliefs and make room for new truths. I had always held the opinion that someone who was gay had either done something horrible to make them this way or something horrible had happened to them. My eyes were opened as I listened to my son pour out his heart to me. He had attended church every Sunday. He'd gone to the weekly activities and served diligently in callings. He'd earned his Duty to God Award and was an Eagle Scout. He'd graduated from seminary and served an honorable mission. I felt immense sadness that Sean had dealt with this alone. I felt intense guilt for having no clue as to what my son had been dealing with for most of his life. Anger crept in at God that He had not answered my son's prayers to take this away.

It was hard for me to think about, so I tried *not* to think about Sean being gay; however, that proved nearly impossible. At one level or another, the worry was always there. The angst was always there too. They were both part of that visceral connection and concern that mothers have for the well being of their children.

Scott and I sincerely wanted to help Sean. We also wanted him and each of our children to follow the gospel path. So, like other Latter-day Saint parents might understandably do, we emailed him various Church articles and scriptures that seemed pertinent to his "situation," still viewing it as a "situation."

We thought the articles would bring him comfort and hope instead of realizing that we were only adding to his pain and discouragement. Perhaps it should have been obvious to Scott and me that Sean had already read and re-read everything we'd sent. He knew certain quotes backward and forward. Still, he continued to patiently read them as we sent them.

After enduring it for quite some time, Sean finally told me that he often cried after receiving one of our well-intentioned emails. He knew they came from a place of love. However, they still caused him to feel worse about himself, not better.

Sean did ask us to read the book *No More Goodbyes* by Carol Lynn Pearson. So Scott read the book while I read Ty Mansfield's *In Quiet Desperation*.[5]

Personal story after story helped Scott and me gain greater understanding. As we learned how no one has chosen to be gay, we gained greater empathy. As we learned about rejection at every turn, we increased our desire to be inclusive. Christlike love grew within us and superseded many of our preconceived notions.

I'd heard of Ty Mansfield's story, how he was attracted to other men while trying to reconcile his attractions with his testimony of The Church of Jesus Christ of Latter-day Saints. I was

---

5. Fred Matis, Marilyn Matis, and Ty Mansfield, *In Quiet Desperation: Understanding the Challenge of Same-Gender Attraction* (Salt Lake City: Deseret Book, 2004).

hoping to learn how I could best help Sean stay faithful, naturally wanting him to achieve the goals *I* had envisioned for *him*.

It wasn't until I started reading *In Quiet Desperation* that I realized that Fred and Marilyn Matis coauthored the book. They were the parents of Stuart Matis, the thirty-two-year-old gay man who took his own life on the steps of a stake center in Los Angeles back in 2000. I remembered the tragic incident, because it was all over the news.

Stuart had described the emotional pain he'd experienced for more than twenty years, saying his knees had become calloused from spending so many long hours in unanswered prayer. He finally decided his life was not worth living. I sobbed as I considered the internal struggle Stuart faced.

It became even more gut wrenching as I thought about how my own son had been wrestling with such a deep emotional and spiritual pain. Stuart's parents loved him, and he knew they loved him. But that still wasn't enough to keep him on this earth. The idea of such an outcome for our family was incomprehensible.

Then I remembered the evening Sean had told me that he had suicidal thoughts several times while growing up. Teens are at high risk for suicide, and LGBTQ youth even more so. It didn't really sink in that it was truly a possibility for us until I read about Stuart. I felt myself going numb with shock. When I finished reading, I called Sean. I pleaded with him to promise he would let me know if he had any more suicidal thoughts. I couldn't fathom life without him.

Ty's story was different. He'd faced a great deal of opposition also with regard to his testimony and attractions to men. However, he was still seeking to find peace while trying to stay faithful to the gospel. One paragraph in particular stood out for me:

I'm learning to put more faith in the love and mercy and understanding of God's judgment and less in my own. I have a great compassion for how difficult trials can be, but I don't think I would have learned the lessons I have had I not been blessed with this trial. Yes, as crazy as it might sound, I have come to feel that on some level my experience with same-gender attraction has been an important blessing for my life. That recognition doesn't make the trial any easier, and there are still times when I weep, wondering when the fight will end, but at least I am beginning to recognize the incredible good that has resulted from my experience.[6]

I wanted to reach through the pages, give Ty a big hug, and thank him for being so vulnerable in sharing his journey. Though he was only twenty-six years old when he wrote *In Quiet Desperation*, he was a wise soul. His experience made me wonder if maybe someday our family might see all of this as a blessing. At the time, it seemed like anything but a blessing.

I learned some important lessons early on: (1) people do not simply choose to be attracted to the same sex, and (2) no two people have the same journey even with similar circumstances. Still, Ty's story left me with renewed hope that it was possible for someone who is attracted to the same sex (like my son) to find peace and fulfillment in the gospel. I wanted so much for Sean to find that.

Scott continued having difficulty accepting the fact that *his* son was gay. He admitted to his own homophobia while insisting Sean's situation was somehow different. He knew of our son's strong spirit and assumed that because of that, his same-sex attractions would surely go away. Scott mistakenly thought that such attractions were directly tied to a person's spiritual strength.

As we continued our quest for greater understanding, I searched for answers to my prayers like Jacob wrestling with the

---

6. Matis, Matis, and Mansfield, *In Quiet Desperation*, 220.

angel (Genesis 32:24). I wouldn't give up hope. I prayed for peace, guidance, and direction so I would know how to help our son.

Some days I found myself sobbing uncontrollably as I grieved the loss of the future I thought my son would have. I hurt to the core as I contemplated the possibility of him never having a traditional nuclear family and never marrying in the temple.

Not only did I grieve the loss of the life I envisioned for my son, I also grieved for him because of the judgment and rejection he had received in the past and would face in the future. It nearly killed me to realize that, even though unwittingly, some of that judgment and rejection had come from me.

I worried about how Sean would fit in, not only in the Church but also in society. Would people be unkind? Would they think less of him? Would they think less of me?

I longed for understanding while so much was unknown. I had countless questions without answers, and part answers I needed to question.

I spent a lot of time in prayer, attending the temple, and pondering what I should do. Admittedly, more than anything, I wanted Sean's same-sex attractions to just go away so things could go back to "normal." I wanted to hear Sean say that no matter how difficult life got, he would stay committed to the gospel and never act on his same-sex attractions. I wanted him to be open to the possibility of falling in love with a woman and marrying her in the temple—like it says in his patriarchal blessing. I wanted the Latter-day Saint fairy tale, the happily ever after ending, or middle, or whatever it was.

Scott and I naively continued to send Sean scriptures and quotes that we felt sure would bring him peace. (Yes, even after he said they weren't helpful, I hate to confess.) I called and texted Sean often, ending every conversation with "I love you." I truly thought I was doing it right and prayed that Sean would also see it that way.

Sean ended every conversation with "I love you too, Mom."

He never complained or argued and seemed to take everything in stride—just like he always did—or so I thought.

Perhaps such misunderstanding helped me endure those first few months after Sean came out to us as gay. Looking back, I'm not sure how we made it through. It was during this time of struggle and heartache that I learned, in a very personal way, that no one cares more about us than our Heavenly Parents. The more aware I became of Their divine love for me, my son, and our family, the more I felt that spirit of charity swelling up within me and enlarging my soul like never before (Alma 32).

I finally realized that before I could help my son, I needed to gain a more divine perspective. I needed to have faith and trust in the power of heaven. That finally made more sense than thinking I could—or should—somehow affect the outcome. Just steal a little bit of my son's agency, I guess. I had no idea of what the future was really going to look like for our son anyway, not to mention the rest of our children.

As I saw how my fears were negatively impacting my entire family, I finally turned them over to God. I stopped insisting on trying to control those things I had no right or ability to control. I remembered that my son was our Heavenly Parent's son long before he came to live with Scott and me. They were watching over him in ways I could not, using insights impossible for me to have at this point in my eternal progression.

I can't count how often I have put my fears at the Savior's feet. Sometimes they are new fears, and other times they are old. Regardless, it is Christ's perfect love that "casteth out *all* fear" (Moroni 8:16). Not just my paralyzed fears, but also my ignorance, frustration, anger, naiveté, and all of it. I've gotten better at placing my burdens at the Savior's feet. Christ has wiped away my tears and comforted my soul. His invitation is direct and promising: "Come unto me, all ye that labour and are heavy laden, and I will give you rest. Take my yoke upon you, and learn of me; for I am meek and lowly in heart: and ye shall find rest unto your souls" (Matthew 11:29–30).

Chapter Three

DIFFERENT BRANCHES OF THE FAMILY TREE: SHARING HARD FAMILY NEWS

Children need to know they can trust your confidence—and your calmness—in any situation. Respect their feelings and their inexperience. Children need to feel safe bringing up the everyday issues as well as the not-so-easy topics such as dating, pornography, friends, sex, money, and more.[7]

Text received from Sean on April Fools' Day: "Mom, is today a good day to tell my siblings I'm gay?"

My immediate return text: "No, not today! It's April Fools'. They won't believe you!"

---

7. The Church of Ziontology, "How to Be a Better Parent." See ziontologist .org/beliefs/parenting.html; accessed July 11, 2019.

"Ha ha. I forgot. So, what day would be good?" Sean was good-natured about it.

"*No* day would be a good day to tell them." I regret that my response was not good-natured.

"Why not?" Sean genuinely wondered why I objected.

"Because it's such devastating news!"

Right after I sent that text, I wished I hadn't.

Sean did not text back.

I knew he had wanted to tell his siblings that he was gay ever since he'd told Scott and me. I was harboring fear at the thought of him telling his siblings. Sean told me he had felt a weight lifted from his shoulders after he came out to his father and me. I knew keeping this from his siblings was another weight he wanted lifted. Now I felt that weight on my shoulders, and I didn't want to place it on my children's shoulders. I felt it would be burdensome for them to know this about their brother. I was still hoping he'd change his mind. I was even naively hoping maybe his attractions would change. (Please let it be a phase.)

After rereading my last text, I felt even more remorse. How could I have been so heartless? I'd given no forethought to how hurtful my seemingly matter-of-fact words could be. Somehow, in my mind, I figured he'd understand. After all, there was still a part of me that felt I had some sort of obligation to make sure he knew I disapproved—as if he hadn't already felt enough disapproval in his life.

And what was I disapproving of? That my son was gay? As if it were his choice to have such attractions? I was already learning such was not the case. Even if it were, and even if he had been acting on his attractions, did I really think he questioned whether I had a testimony of The Church of Jesus Christ of Latter-day Saints and a modern-day prophet? Did I really need to remind him of that yet again?

Actually, there was one of his siblings I'd wanted Sean to tell: his oldest brother, Tosh. They shared a close, brotherly bond. Tosh was wise and deeply spiritual. I thought maybe Tosh could reach Sean in a way that Scott and I had been unable to. Again, because I was still so new at this, I didn't even think about how much it would help Sean to feel love from his older brother no matter what. I'd also been hoping Tosh could help "change Sean's mind" (as if it were simply a matter of changing one's mind).

Tosh was serving a mission in London when Sean was a senior in high school. He'd been preparing to send in his own mission papers after graduating, so we thought it would be meaningful to take him with us to pick up Tosh from his mission. While we were in Europe, we also visited Scotland where Scott had served his mission twenty-five years earlier. The four of us had an amazing two weeks together. The summer after we returned, Tosh and Sean flew to New York to tour the Church historical sites before Sean left for his mission.

I thought, *If anyone could help Sean keep an eternal perspective, Tosh could.* After we first learned about Sean being gay, I asked him if he felt ready to tell Tosh. If not, I wanted permission to tell him. Sean said he didn't feel ready and that he wanted to tell all six of his siblings at the same time. He felt it wouldn't be fair to have Tosh know and not his other brothers and sisters.

Scott and I felt good about Sean telling Tosh, but we had reservations about other siblings. We were pretty sure two of our children would be very supportive of him dating other men (and, of course I wanted none of that). We were also concerned that some of his other siblings would be outright devastated (forgetting that our kids' and grandkids' generations are far more accepting of same-sex couples).

A few days after April Fools', Scott and I stopped by Tosh's house to help him in his yard. I started talking to Tosh about a few family matters, and before I knew it, the words just spilled out of my mouth: "Sean is gay."

Tosh was taken aback. As he thought about it, things started to make sense. He'd wondered why Sean wasn't interested in dating girls when so many had been interested in him. There were several Tosh had thought would be perfect for Sean. At the time, the idea that it was because Sean was gay didn't cross his mind.

I asked Tosh to ponder and pray about how to best approach Sean, hoping he wouldn't be upset that I'd told his brother. I planned to call Sean that evening, but Tosh beat me to it. He called while Sean was enjoying dinner out with some friends. When he learned I'd spilled the beans, it caught him completely off guard. Sean just listened as Tosh told him he loved him. If only Tosh had stopped right there (again, the benefit of hindsight). Instead, Tosh took off in the same direction Scott and I had been going. He shared a spiritually based story that he thought would boost Sean's faith and trust in God. Instead, it crushed his heart and weakened his trust in me.

Sean returned home early and called me. He was hurt and upset. He couldn't believe I'd told Tosh without his permission. I tried to justify my actions, hoping he would see that it was all for the best. You might think it was actually for *my* best, but in reality, it was for no one's best. I begged Sean for forgiveness. I realized I had betrayed my son's confidence, and for that I was deeply sorry.

I wished I could have taken it back. I wished I could have taken quite a few things back. I struggled, feeling I was failing Sean and failing as a mother. Nothing hurts more, matters more, or brings more joy or sorrow to me than being a mother to my kids. It's such a heavy responsibility and an amazing privilege. I was so hard on myself when, in reality, none of us really knew the best ways to handle such a new and foreign experience.

Sean wanted all his siblings to know at the same time, and I'd taken that away from him. He felt forced to tell his other siblings since I'd told Tosh. The following day, Sean courageously sent a coming-out email to each of his other siblings. More than anything, he hoped they would continue to love him and treat him the same.

He wrote, "I want to be completely honest with you, because I love you so much. I want to have an honest relationship with my family." Then he proceeded to disclose what he had worked hard—at great personal expense—to keep secret for so many years.

Five of his six other siblings called him shortly after receiving his email. With empathy and compassion, they expressed their love for their brother. Our daughter Myley recalls, "For a split second, I thought it was a belated April Fools' joke. I skimmed over it looking for the punch line. Then I opened a video he said would help explain things. I watched for just a few seconds before I realized he was truly coming out to me. Somehow it had never crossed my mind. I called him immediately and said I felt bad that he had to hear so many terrible things growing up. I felt sad for him, knowing there might be some family and friends who weren't going to be supportive. I told him how much I loved him and supported him."

Sean recalls waiting four days before his last sibling finally responded. Those four days filled him with much anxiety, and he experienced several panic attacks. He'd grown up keeping this huge secret, and for so many years, his greatest fear was that others might find out he was gay. Now that fear was being played out on the battlefield, and he wasn't sure if anyone was fighting on his side. The coming out process filled him with such angst. Sure, he was relieved to finally tell family; however, he was deathly afraid of what the fallout might be.

The last of his siblings finally called, and his greatest fear was realized—being judged for who he was. Sean said she called bawling like he had died or something. The only thing he remembered her saying was, "We're supposed to be a celestial family! Don't you want us to be together in the celestial kingdom? You're making it so we can't be a together family."

Of course, he remembered those words. They seared straight through to his soul. My dear, kind-hearted daughter loved Sean and truly thought she was helping. My dear, kind-hearted son loved our family and had feared just such a fate: the thought that there was something so inherently wrong with him that he wouldn't be able to be with his family in the celestial kingdom.

She'd unintentionally broken his heart. He broke down in tears that day and so many days and months that followed. He continued to deal with overwhelming anxiety and panic attacks. He didn't feel supported by anyone and didn't know where to turn.

Looking back, I wish I could have focused less on my own fear and pain so I could have helped Sean through his. However, I was so strongly affected by it all that I simply could not do more. I truly did my best, missteps and all.

The coming out process can be so overwhelming, confusing, and emotional for all involved. I felt bad that my daughter, whom I love dearly, was so upset. I felt bad that my son, whom I also love dearly, was so distraught. It was a learning and growing process for our entire family, and it came with many learning and growing pains.

Chapter Four

A HOUSE DIVIDED

"If I'm Accepting of My LGBTQ Child, Exactly What Am I Accepting?"

"Do I love and support my church?" or *"Do I love and support my child who has a same-sex partner?"* We can do both.[8]

—*Elder Dale G. Renlund*

Several years ago, Elder Dallin H. Oaks received a letter from an upset parent. What deeply moved him the most was when the parent said, "After I found out my son is gay . . . I forbad him to come to our home, and I cut him off and said he's not my son anymore."

Elder Oaks replied, "That's just not acceptable behavior on the part of a parent, and in a loving relationship, and even in the

---

8. Dale G. Renlund, Western Regional Conference, February 14, 2016.

public square." He then encouraged that parent to repent and reestablish a loving relationship with the child.[9]

It's one thing to imagine how you might react if one of your children started dating a member of the same sex and wanted to bring him or her home for dinner. It's quite another to actually get a text from your child saying precisely that.

I'll never forget the day my son texted me to let me know he was dating a guy. And not just any guy. This was someone he really cared about. Someone he wanted to bring over for dinner to meet the family. Our family!

I was well aware that Sean might try dating a guy at some point in his life. Of course, I held out hope he might avoid such relationships. I also hoped he might try dating women again. (As if those attractions would magically appear.) I didn't know Sean had been dating, much less dating someone he cared about enough to invite to family dinner and bring into *our* home.

The possibility I'd been cloaking with deniability was suddenly exposed with a blinding flash of reality, a reality for which I was so inadequately prepared. The dizziness hit just as surprisingly. I felt nauseous as the memory from two years prior came flooding back when I had told our kids that if Sean started dating men, he would not be allowed to bring the date into our home. I was so concerned about the example he would be setting for my kids and grandkids.

"Mom, that is so wrong!" Two of our children immediately jumped to Sean's defense. "You allowed us to bring our friends and dates home. It's only fair that you let Sean do the same thing. We can't push him away! Telling him that will make him feel rejected. You've always taught us how important it is to support each other as a family."

---

9. Dallin H. Oaks, *Tribtalk*, with Jennifer Napier-Pearce, January 29, 2015.

"Hey, wait a minute!" Another child weighed in. "I totally disagree! You've always taught us how important it is to be obedient and to set a good example for others—especially our own children. Accepting Sean's choices goes against all of that! Marriage is supposed to be between a man and a woman! We don't want our kids exposed to homosexuality. Then they might start wondering what's right and what's wrong. How confusing is that?"

The discussion heated up quickly. It was my first glimpse of our family divided over the very thought of dating. Now it was a reality.

I read Sean's text again. Then I got upset. Really upset. I thought, *How could Sean do this to me? Why didn't he prepare me? And how can he tell me he has a boyfriend in a text?*

Now I can see his wisdom in messaging/texting me news I'd find upsetting. The texts meant he wouldn't have to see or hear my initial reaction. Something else we are both very grateful for. Sean was looking out for my feelings. I hate to admit it, but I was usually looking out for my feelings too.

I calmed down a little before starting my response. Then I said a quick prayer.

"Please, Heavenly Father. How do I handle this? What should I say?"

I had a sense of just how significant my response to Sean would be. He'd kindly (and I do mean kindly) explained to me what was hurtful about my response when I learned he was gay. Throughout the entire experience, the presence of the Holy Spirit helped us open up rather than close down. The Spirit called to remembrance the deep, deep love I have for all my children, and for Sean in particular.

Objecting would be hurtful. But accepting would be, well, accepting. I repeated a similar prayer several times, because I was perturbed by the answer. It was the same message I'd been getting all along: "Love him. Love him no matter what."

Impatiently, I argued back, "This is different. He wants to bring his boyfriend into *our* home."

Again, a kind and patient response: "Love him. Love him no matter what." I knew what that meant. I knew it meant that I should tell Sean that anyone he loved was welcome in our home.

"Seriously?"

I had so many questions that weren't being answered. Or so many answers I didn't want questioned. I searched for peace as I considered many of the ramifications of "allowing" Sean to bring his boyfriend to our next family dinner. Still, the Lord blessed me with a clear answer, so I moved forward with more faith and less fear.

I took a deep breath as I texted Sean back. "Yes, of course."

Right after that, I called Scott. I wondered why I didn't call him before texting Sean back. However, I knew by his response that I'd done things in the right order. He nervously replied, "I hope this doesn't divide our family." If he'd said that beforehand, I doubt I could have moved forward. He would have confirmed my fears, not my faith.

But here it was, staring me right in the face.

I took a deep breath and sent out a group text to my other six children, letting them know Sean was bringing a guy—someone he really cared about—to our family dinner to meet the family.

Unfortunately, when the hypothetical discussion about Sean dating other young men became a reality, the concerns of some family members intensified—in opposite directions. One of my children and their spouse insisted that if we were to include Sean's boyfriend that would be setting a bad example. Kids and grandkids would think we were actively supporting gay relationships. They reminded me that I'd held this same point of view, and now it felt as if I were betraying them and God. They felt I was choosing Sean's boyfriend over my own grandchildren. That one really hurt.

Their hurt and frustration over our change of perspective caused me great hurt and frustration too. I don't want any of my children to suffer. I empathized with them and their concerns for their own children, because I'd felt the same way about them—my own children. The thought of some of my kids refusing to come to certain family events tore my heart in two. However, I could not deny the witness from the Holy Spirit that Scott and I needed to love and include all of our children as best we could. I knew the others were doing what they felt was best for their family. I sought to be respectful of them, their agency, and their perspective—even though their answers were different from mine.

The morning of the family dinner, Sean called to tell me how nervous he and his invited guest were to come to dinner. He wanted reassurance that no one was going to say something hurtful. I was ashamed that Sean would think that we would intentionally say something mean or cruel. I assured him we'd all be kind. I too was nervous, but for another reason. I wondered how it would feel to see my son with a man he was dating.

I was busy preparing dinner in the kitchen when I heard Sean pull into the driveway. I nervously went into the family room to greet him and his boyfriend. As Sean introduced his boyfriend, my initial thought was, "What a nice young man." He was polite and gracious. I'm not sure what I was expecting him to be or why I was pleasantly surprised when I saw how nice he was—I just was. After dinner, we played games until late in the evening. I hugged each of my children and Sean's date goodbye as they parted for home.

The following morning, Sean called to see how I thought the evening had gone. I said, "I think it went very well. I just thought of him as your friend having dinner with us."

He said, "Mom, when you say things like that it really hurts. He's more than a friend. I really care about him."

I replied, "Sean, be patient, it's not easy for me to wrap my brain around this. I'm still processing."

I had to resist the urge to even hint at disapproval. Sean was so sensitive to it. And he could easily recognize when we'd use it in an effort to manipulate his choices.

Not once did Heavenly Father tell me to shun, shame, or show disapproval of Sean. I did anyway, more times than I care to admit. Needless to say, it never turned out well. Contention would creep into my thoughts and then my heart. Wedges would form. Defenses would build. Trust would dwindle.

The summer after Sean graduated from BYU–Hawaii and entered the masters program at the University of Hawaii, he and his boyfriend moved in together around the same time our youngest daughter moved in with her boyfriend. Though these changes were not a complete shock, they were two hard pills to swallow. Scott and I couldn't help but feel we were failing as parents. I wondered, "What's happening to my eternal family? Where is the joy in family life?"

My emotions were all over the place. I felt anger, sadness, and grief. My mind whirled with questions for God: "Who has the greater sin? My son or my daughter?" Once again, we were desperately trying to navigate uncharted territory. I was getting seasick and wanted to help steady the ship but didn't know how.

As a mother and a member of The Church of Jesus Christ of Latter-day Saints, my hope has always been for the welfare of our children. I wanted them to walk the gospel path, the one path that has brought peace to my soul. Yet, I have spent many nights unable to sleep, tossing and turning with worry for my children. Oftentimes I'd get back up and fall to my knees, seeking guidance and comfort through prayer, or seek solace and answers in the scriptures.

That's when I truly began to notice that the scriptures are filled with imperfect individuals and families—parents and children—who navigate challenges in ways that aren't all that different from our own. Adam and Eve, whose son Cain murdered his brother Abel (we didn't have that problem, thank goodness); Lehi and Sariah, whose two older sons rebelled; Abraham, Isaac, and Jacob, those towering figures who, with their wives, experienced much parental sorrow; Alma the Younger, who had a rebellious son, Corianton; and Mosiah, who had a few rebellious sons.[10] The scriptures describe some "happy endings" for those who journeyed with God, and that's what I wanted for our family: A happy ending.

My heart was softened as I thought about each of our children and their significant other. I felt an overwhelming desire for all of us to be together as a family, united in love. I also thought about Lehi and his vision, when he partook of the fruit of the tree of life and "began to be desirous that my family should partake of it also; for I knew that it was desirable above all other fruit" (1 Nephi 8:12).

Scott was having a tough time wrapping his mind around our children's living arrangements. He was pretty upset, so I reminded him, "Scott, you know we have to love and embrace our children and their boyfriends. Otherwise, they won't want to be here or have anything to do with us. Their boyfriends won't want to come here or ever learn about our church if the very people they see as churchgoers are some of the most judgmental and cruel."

I quickly added, "We have to love. Our children know our values. They know our perspective. But if we want a relationship with our children, we need to respect their agency."

Scott agreed. He knew it was our best chance at bringing our family closer together and keeping them that way.

---

10. See John H. Carmack, "When Our Children Go Astray," *Ensign*, February 1997.

As time went on, some of our children still chose not to attend certain family gatherings. They were greatly missed. Family gatherings weren't the same. It was a stressful and pain-filled time. I prayed and pleaded with God for answers on how to bring my family together in spite of differences.

When I visited with my children who were opting out, they continued to tell me they did not approve of our decision to open our door to all. I tried to say things that might soften their hearts and create more unity. I even shared articles and scriptures—I suppose in a manner similar to how I'd been sharing with Sean after he first came out to us. That often led to more division and hurt feelings.

At some point, I realized I'd been trying to change their perspective and how they lived their lives. Yes, sharing such things might be good in some instances. However, I soon learned to be more prayerful and circumspect. I quit insisting on my own point of view and sending articles that supported what I thought. I learned to avoid sounding preachy, judgmental, or like I was talking down to any of my kids. I realized that to some extent I was being manipulative in an effort to get them to respond in ways I wanted them to. Those discussions led to arguments, contention, and frustration, which caused even more pain and division.

I sought personal revelation through frequent trips to the temple and constantly being on my knees, which brought peace and reassurance that it would all work out. I didn't know how things would work out, but I had to trust that God did. I was doing my best in the best way I knew how.

We continued to extend the invitation for all of our children to be respectful toward anyone who chose not to attend. When I was finally able to step back and look at things with a more objective and inspired perspective, I realized that all of us were coming from a place of integrity—that which we felt was best for our individual families.

One evening, after another family gathering with empty chairs at the table, I was feeling especially frustrated and discouraged, because I couldn't seem to find the right words to say or figure out how to say what I thought without creating bigger holes in the knitting project that was my family.

After everyone went home, I sat down at my computer to check my emails, and a subject line from *LDS Living Magazine* caught my eye: "Pres. Monson Gives Important Caution for Latter-day Saints." It read in part:

> We've all felt anger. It can come when things don't turn out the way we want. It might be a reaction to something which is said of us or to us. We may experience it when people don't behave the way we want them to behave. Perhaps it comes when we have to wait for something longer than we expected. We might feel angry when others can't see things from our perspective. There seem to be countless possible reasons for anger. . . .
>
> To be angry is to yield to the influence of Satan. No one can *make* us angry. It is our choice. If we desire to have a proper spirit with us at all times, we must choose to refrain from becoming angry. I testify that such is possible.[11]

This article came at the perfect time. It shared an example of a family divided that over time was able to come to a place of understanding, a place of forgiveness, and join together in loyalty and unity. It was just what I needed, and it turned out to be just what our family needed also. I sent the article to my kids, telling them that it had touched my heart. I received a heartfelt reply the next day: "Thank you for sharing this article. I didn't know if things would ever be better. But after reading our Prophet's message, I know it will be better. I love you too, Mom."

---

11. Thomas S. Monson, "School Thy Feelings, O My Brother," *Ensign*, November 2009.

The Prophet spoke gospel truths, and the Holy Ghost confirmed those truths, allowing them to sink deep into our hearts. We loved each other and wanted to be together. We sought to turn to Christ and reach for the healing power of the Atonement. Where there was anger, there began to be greater understanding and a renewed desire to open our hearts and our homes. The hearts of each family member was softened and strengthened in the Lord's timing.

Scott and I learned to respect our children's agency and choices—whether it was Sean choosing to bring a date to a family event, or other children choosing to avoid the family event altogether. We have always encouraged our children to be mindful of different perspectives and respond to one another with respect and kindness. We emphasized that our door would be open to everyone—each member of our family—and extended family had the same invitation to our gatherings. While we hoped all would come, we knew some would not. It hurt when anyone was missing.

I am grateful they all walk through the door now with love and respect. I have learned to turn a great deal more over to the Lord than I used to. The older I get, the more I realize how comprehensive the principles of faith and sacrifice truly are. Through our trust and faith in the Lord, we are willing to put everything at his feet, including that which buoys us up, and that which seeks to drag us down. The Lord is always there, waiting to help us along.

Some days were still hard. I did my best to look for the good, and there was plenty of it. We received personal messages from LGBTQ individuals about how every step of their journey was filled with depression, anxiety, and suicidal ideation. Theirs was a history of rejection and/or the fear of rejection, even for those who hadn't necessarily acted on their attractions. Every time I received a heartbreaking message, I was relieved that Sean had come out to his father and me. I was grateful for his trust in us, our good relationship, and our eternal family circle.

When my son moved in with his boyfriend and my daughter moved in with her boyfriend, our decision to move forward with love and inclusion has kept the lines of communication open. It has brought our family continued opportunities to grow together in new ways.

Our daughter's boyfriend is now our son-in-law, and we love him dearly. If we'd been cold or even lukewarm with him, things might have worked out differently. That's a sad thought. Our son and his first boyfriend are no longer together. It was a tough breakup for us as well as our son, because we loved him too.

"Kindness is the power that God has given us to unlock hard hearts and subdue stubborn souls."[12]

I finally realized that my stubborn soul was the one in need of bowing more fully to God's will—whatever that might be.

---

12. *Teachings of Presidents of the Church—George Albert Smith*, "The Power of Kindness" (Salt Lake City: The Church of Jesus Christ of Latter-day Saints, 2011). See pages 225–28 and churchofjesuschrist.org/study/manual/teachings-george-albert-smith/chapter-21?lang=eng; accessed July 15, 2019.

Chapter Five

GREATER UNDERSTANDING: SHARING LIFE LESSONS LEARNED

Faith, hope, and charity complement each other, and as one increases, the others grow as well. Hope comes of faith, for without faith, there is no hope. In like manner faith comes of hope, for faith is "the substance of things hoped for."[13]

—Elder Dieter F. Uchtdorf

I must admit that one of the first concerns I had when Sean told me he was gay was that he might contract and even die from HIV/AIDS. My fears stemmed from hearing the reports on the news concerning the rampant growth of HIV/AIDS in the United States in the 1980s. Because homosexual men were considered to be at high risk for AIDS, and because knowledge of the disease was limited, many associated the disease with homosexual activity. I was well aware of the negative stigma tied to gays.

---

13. Dieter F. Uchtdorf, "The Infinite Power of Hope," *Ensign*, November 2008.

Worse yet, I'd heard some people propose that AIDS was God's way of punishing gays. I'm not sure what they thought about the heterosexual people and children who also contracted the disease, not to mention countless other diseases that can affect anyone at any time.

When I expressed my fear to Sean, he patiently reminded me that we live in a time when there has been much progress surrounding the treatment and prevention of the disease. I was grateful that even more common misunderstandings were put to rest at the end of 2012, a year after Sean told us he was gay. The Church launched the original Mormons and Gays website. I was elated that the Church had a website dedicated to increase understanding and emphasizing the importance to love one another. One of my greatest fears was how people would treat Sean if they knew this about him. Having a website with videos from the Apostles, would they now be respectful and kind? This question was at the forefront of my mind.

The purpose for the website was summed up: "In an effort to encourage understanding and civil conversation about same-sex attraction, The Church of Jesus Christ of Latter-day Saints has launched the website Love One Another: A Discussion on Same-Sex Attraction (www.mormonsandgays.org)."[14]

In one of the videos on the website, I was so touched when Elder Quentin L. Cook talked about serving as stake president in San Francisco in the 1980s during the AIDS epidemic:

> Clearly the hardest thing I had when I was stake president [was] . . .
> we had 17 men with AIDS and at that point, there was no cure. All
> 17 of them ultimately died of AIDS while I was stake president. . . .

---

14. Mormon News Room, "New Church Website on Same-Sex Attraction Offers Love, Understanding and Hope," December 6, 2012. See newsroom .churchofjesuschrist.org/article/church-website-same-sex-attraction; accessed July 15, 2019.

I watched bishops who made incredible sacrifices to take care of some of these young men who were dying . . . I watched them take care of each other. And I watched some of them, one of them comes to mind in particular, a returned missionary, in a single incidence of conduct, took it upon himself to take care of the most difficult situations, those that were the most ill, and he was the last one to die.[15]

It was heartbreaking to hear that so many of our Latter-day Saint brothers died of AIDS and that their parents and family members had to grieve the loss of their loved one. I was grateful to know of the progress of prevention and treatment of AIDS. Still, in the back of mind, the fear lingered that one day it could be my son or someone I know and love in the LGBTQ community dying of AIDS. I've come to the conclusion that a mother never truly stops worrying about her children. Ever. I pray that no more parents experience the loss of a child in such a way. Education and prevention is vital.

The Mormon and Gay website also contained statements, resources, and videos of love, understanding, and hope. I felt it was a great start and would help people become more comfortable talking about LGBTQ matters with other Church members. I was grateful that Church leaders were finally publicly addressing the subject. The more I listened to others' stories, the more love and compassion I felt, not only for my son, but also for others going through similar circumstances.

The website expanded knowledge too. It stated, "The experience of same-sex attraction is a complex reality for many people," and "individuals do not choose to have such attractions." I was relieved to see the Church acknowledge that same-sex attraction is a complex issue and that it isn't something a person simply chooses to experience. I hoped that statement would help people

15. Quentin L. Cook, "Let Us Be at the Forefront." See mormonandgay. churchofjesuschrist.org/articles/love-one-another-a-discussion-on-same-sex-attraction?lang=eng; accessed July 15, 2019.

understand that being gay doesn't indicate a lack faith or a lack of effort to "rid themselves" of such attractions.

I asked my kids to visit the site so they could gain a greater understanding. I also asked Sean if he and I could watch some of the videos from the site together. I quickly learned that he was coming at it from a different perspective. He was afraid that the stories of those LGBTQ individuals who were active Church members, including some who married those of the opposite sex, might be used against him and others. Some people would adopt the false idea that "If they can be faithful and make it work, why can't you?"

As Sean considered such reactions from others and experienced some of it, his feelings of shame, isolation, and pain intensified. As he shared his concerns about the message he felt the videos were sending, I had empathy. I hadn't thought of it from that perspective. I knew he was right, because on the night he came out to me, I had responded by telling him that I had heard of a Latter-day Saint gay man who was married to a woman and was confident that he could be too. I thought it would give Sean hope, but now I realized that it only intensified his fears of being a disappointment. No one wants to be compared to another or to be told if they just had more faith they would no longer be gay.

I did not intend to go public about our family's experiences with Sean. In our Latter-day Saint culture, I questioned why anyone would want to be so open about *this* topic. I didn't understand how we could possibly help anyone by sharing our experiences with having a gay child, until I finished reading Carol Lynn Pearson's book *No More Goodbyes*. I'd tucked it under my bed shortly after Sean first asked me to read it, because it stirred up some intense emotions. Almost two years later, when he asked if I'd finished the book, I admitted I had not but agreed to do so.

As I opened the book and began reading where I had left off, I could barely make out the words through the tears streaming down my face. The pages were filled with riveting stories of Latter-day Saint LGBTQ individuals finally getting the courage to do the scariest thing they had ever done—*come out to their parents!* Their reaction horrified me. Their parents kicked them out! I could not wrap my mind around such an extreme reaction. I couldn't fathom how a parent could justify turning their back on their own child at such a volatile time (or at any time, for any reason). Once out on the street, many turned to substance abuse and/or prostitution to survive, and many took their life to end the pain. Now I was doing the ugly cry! How did our culture become so homophobic that we would turn our own child away? At what point do you ignore the commandment "Love thy neighbor"? The real life scenarios I was reading about made no sense to me. I was furious. As I continued reading, there were other parents who were choosing their child (as they should) but were leaving the Church with the perspective that if there was not a place for their LGBTQ child in the Church, then there was not a place for them. I could not imagine my life without my son or my life without the Church. I did not feel the choice was between one or the other. I was choosing both! As I read on, it became clear that other parents of LGBTQ children were hurting. I realized that these parents were experiencing the same pain and discouragement that Scott and I had experienced, and there weren't many voices out there offering support.

I felt this undeniable call to let others know that "You can do this! It's going to be okay. Don't step away from the Church, and don't turn your back on your LGBTQ child. Embrace both. Love and trust the Lord. Respect your child's agency. You *can* do this!"

I realized I could offer a voice of encouragement and faith for others. I felt a strong impression that it was time to "come out" of my own closet as an active member of The Church of Jesus Christ of Latter-day Saints and the mother of a gay son I loved and adored. Denying his feelings or mine served no one. I was learning the importance of letting parents know they don't have to choose between their testimonies and their gay children. It doesn't have to be a "one or the other" choice. We can embrace both, and the Lord calls us to do so.

As I was feeling the need to publicly reach out to help others, I mustered the courage to tell Sean what the Spirit had impressed upon me and asked if he'd be willing to help. It seemed that the best way to "get the word out" would be to create a video when he came home for Christmas. He could share what it was like to grow up carrying this secret alone and talk about the years he contemplated suicide. I could share what I had been learning as his mother: How important it is to let go of the idea that a child being gay is somehow the parents' "fault," as if blame even needed to be assigned, and LGBTQ individuals are our brothers and sisters (and children), not enemies of God.

Sean thought about the prospect of making a video to help others in an environment that could be hostile from any direction. He said, "Mom, that would really be putting me out there. (Long pause.) But you're right. We could help many people. So, okay, let's do it." That's just how Sean is. He has a good heart, and he emanates care and concern for others. When I told Scott what I felt impressed to do, he was supportive and surprised, because we hadn't been open about this outside of our children. He wasn't going to argue with a prompting. He said he would support Sean and me in doing a video, but as far as him being in it or talking to others about his own experience and journey, he was not to that point yet.

Helped by his sister Kelsey, a film graduate, we shot the video without rehearsing or discussing what we'd say. There was no script of what to say and what *not* to say. After filming a forty-minute interview, we edited it down to six minutes. Mostly, we wanted families who were struggling in silence to realize that they weren't alone.

Up to that point, Sean had only come out to his siblings and closest friends. As we were about to release the video, we didn't want extended family and loved ones to hear about it through social media. So, I emailed them to share our story and why we felt it was right to do so.

I also let our bishop and stake president know what we were planning to do and sought their counsel. We had been in contact with our stake president ever since that first night with Sean, but we hadn't told our bishop. Scott and I met with him in his office and showed him the video and blog article that would soon be public.

In addition to seeking his counsel, I wanted him to be aware of the situation since I was worried he'd get calls from ward members asking questions such as, "What is Sister Mackintosh talking about? Is it okay to talk about this?"

Sure, I'd served as Primary president, Young Women president, and stake Young Women president while currently serving as a seminary teacher. I didn't know how people would perceive me or receive me. Regardless, I knew it was the right thing to do, because the prompting from the Spirit was so strong that I could not ignore it. Knowing that, I sought to let go and let whatever consequences fall as they may. That's easier said than done, of course. I was so nervous. With courage, I moved forward with faith and trust.

We titled the video and blog article *A Very Real Matter: Same-sex Attraction*. Pushing that publish button on our video was one of the scariest things I've ever done. My stomach tied itself in knots as our story went live and we stepped into the often harsh and cruel light of social media. I dug deeper than ever to muster the courage needed to share the link on Facebook and Twitter. I feared negative reactions of friends and strangers, learning in my own way what that was like. Even more so, I feared negative reactions toward my son, unaware of how much there had been already. I sent out a motherly plea for all to invest in kindness.

We published the videos two years to the day from when Sean had sent his father and me his coming out letter. The response was overwhelming, and that's putting it mildly.

Literally hundreds of people from all over the world reached out to us. They shared their own heartbreaking and heartwarming stories, while thanking us for being so raw and real. Parents thanked me for letting them know they weren't traveling this path alone. I was surprised at how many LGBTQ people told me they thought they were the only one in the Church dealing with such feelings and how they had feared telling anyone at all. After seeing our video, they were so grateful to know they were not alone.

The sheer number of responses also overwhelmed us. We knew they were from just a fraction of the total number of Latter-day Saint LGBTQ individuals and family members. For those who replied and for those who stayed silent, we saw a great need for love and support.

As Sean and I slowly made our way through the responses that poured in, we noticed fathers were reaching out to Scott. They asked how he was able to get to a place of peace while loving his son. This helped Scott realize the role he could play in helping fathers and families. It was the nudge he needed, and the Spirit let him know it was time.

One father said, "I just watched your wife's video with your son, and I think I have been doing it wrong. My son came out at the dinner table four years ago, and I told him to get up and get out of my house. I have not spoken to him since." Scott suggested that he send his son a text saying he loves him. "That's a great idea, but if he wants to come home . . ."

Scott interrupted and said, "No, you're not hearing me. Just send him a text, without stipulations, that says 'I love you.' No ifs or buts." Scott was able to share what he'd learned from his own negative reaction to Sean. It was the beginning of a father and son mending a broken relationship as another father and son strengthened theirs.

Another surprise was how many people approached me at church to tell me they had a gay brother, sister, aunt, uncle, cousin, etc. With tears in their eyes, they thanked me for posting the video. One sister told me that our video touched her so much that she reached out to her gay brother that she had not spoken to in years. She asked for forgiveness because of the way she had shunned him and his partner.

It would've been worth it if only one person had been helped by our video. I am amazed at how true that is, especially since it was so difficult. The responses of so many have opened our eyes to the reality of how many families are navigating this same journey and trying to do the best they can in the best way they know how.

Being open about our experiences deepened my understanding of the plan of salvation and the gospel of Jesus Christ. As I bore witness to others of the Savior's love, the Spirit bore witness to me. It changed the way I love my son and our other children, my husband, my neighbors, my Savior, and myself.

My mother often said to me, "When you learn a better way, commit to do better." It's not always easy, because we are creatures of habit, and we seek to keep our private lives private. However, one of the greatest things I have learned from "coming out" is that when I respond to people and situations from a place of love, things typically turn out better. We may not be able to alter the journey, but we can make sure no one walks it alone.

There have been times when I have not spoken up and wished I had. Not in an effort to criticize others, but to increase understanding. I was talking with some fellow Church members when they began to share their concerns and fears about the way the world was moving toward its acceptance of the LGBTQ community and same-sex marriage. I wanted to join in the conversation and steer it toward greater compassion, but I was I still feeling guarded about what to share, when to share it, and how it might be received.

One person commented, "I don't know how I would react if a child of mine told me they were gay." Then he shuddered in disgust as another expressed similar concerns. I thought about what I would say. Perhaps something like, "I am a mother who has a son who told me he was gay, and the first thing I told him was that I loved him. It takes courage to come out, especially to tell a parent, and if you ever have a child tell you they're gay, it's really important to respond with love and kindness. They need to know, more than anything, that you love them."

I couldn't verbalize my thoughts before the conversation ended. I knew they were speaking from a place of fear, because they lacked understanding. They feared having their own children venture off the path to pursue a life different than what they had planned for them. (It's easy to think we *can* plan for their futures.) Their comments reflected the same perspective I had before someone I loved more than life itself told me he was gay.

I've reflected on that day many times, and it has increased my desire to take opportunities to teach—and learn—as they come along. A desire for greater understanding is of God. I look for more opportunities to share when the spirit urges me to do so. I resolve to be bolder and more loving in acting upon impressions to testify when and where the Spirit prompts.

I love Sister Chieko N. Okazaki, who served as a counselor in the general Relief Society presidency years ago. She said,

> How much courage does it take in a Relief Society class to raise your hand when everyone seems to agree on only one point of view but where it seems to contradict the Savior's law of love? Who will

represent the point of view of people like you if you do not? Who will speak for your children if you do not? Who will speak for kindness and justice and mercy? If the Spirit whispers that there are people who need to hear your voice, then try to find a way to speak—not to criticize or to force a different decision but to share your perspective. The Church needs to hear the voices of all its members—the voices of its women, its people of color, its new converts, its handicapped members, its divorced members, its teenagers and children, its mothers with small children, its priesthood leaders trying to help. It needs to hear from people who struggle with mental illness, with same-sex attraction, with poverty, and with sorrow.[16]

I'm grateful that Sister Okazaki always cared enough to share. She not only defended diversity, she also praised it. Little did I know that years later her words would have great meaning for me. Her willingness to share strengthened me. I hope that in turn, my sharing can strengthen others. After all, that is how the gospel is designed to work.

16. Chieko N. Okazaki, *What a Friend We Have in Jesus* (Salt Lake City: Deseret Book, 2008), 84.

Chapter Six

PARENTS AND CHILDREN, SHARING AND SUPPORTING

But ye will teach them to walk in the ways of truth and sober-ness; ye will teach them to love one another, and to serve one another.

— *King Benjamin (Mosiah 4:15)*

Children often take their cues from their parents with regard to a family member coming out as gay. They are likely to sense a parent's anxiety or unwillingness to accept their sibling. In contrast, they can also feel their parents' love and support. It is important for all of our children to feel they are safe and that their parents will always love them—no matter what they have done. If our children see us rejecting certain family members because they aren't following the path we think they should follow, this can give our other kids, and grandkids, the impression that they could be rejected too.

President Ezra Taft Benson said, "Encourage your children to come to you . . . with their problems and questions by listening to them every day."[17]

Parents often ask how young is too young to tell younger children or grandchildren about their brother (or sister or cousin) coming out as LGBTQ? They worry about the message they'll be sending their younger children or grandchildren. Unfortunately, there is not a one-size-fits-all answer. But I am confident with the formula of pondering, praying, and acting upon the impressions you receive.

My friend Rachel and her husband Jonathan Manwarring were great examples of seeking inspiration ahead of time as they prepared to tell their five young children that their favorite uncle was gay. They included Uncle Jamison in their family circle, and he's an important part of their family.

Rachel wrote an online article about how they handled the situation:

> We began by talking in general terms about gay people. We started asking questions around the dinner table like, "Do you know what gay means?" "Have you ever known anyone who is gay?"
>
> When it came time for us to tell our children, we weren't scared. We gathered our children around and watched (Jamison's) video. They were unfazed and were just happy to be seeing his smiling face. . . .[18]

Your love for your fellowmen will not turn the rest of your children gay. It's not contagious. It is not something you can make happen or keep from happening. It's part of their journey

---

17. Ezra Taft Benson, "The Honored Place of Women," *Ensign*, November 1981.

18. Rachel Manwarring, "And What Do You Teach Your Children?" See lds-lights.org/teach-children; accessed July 16, 2019.

in this life. Why? We don't know why. It's not our job to know why. Our job is to love.

A mother recently told me that when her oldest daughter told her she was lesbian, her first instinct was that she had to protect her six younger children. She said, "Suddenly, it became 'her' and 'us.'" She said she went into a frantic fear mode and started setting all sorts of boundaries, because she "couldn't allow anything like that in my house." Then she said she took to heart my advice: "Your family is going to mimic your response. Your kids need to see that their big sister is the same great person that she was yesterday before she came out." She said that this was the message she wanted to share with her other children—to treat their sister the same. The mother said she felt peace, yet irresponsible somehow to not do something to control the situation. Then she realized that it is "the magic of faith" to let go of what you cannot control and let Heavenly Father take care of it. That's really what it boils down to—responding from a place of love, letting go of what you cannot control, and turning it over to God and the Savior.

Remember that it can be scary for Latter-day Saint LGBTQ individuals to open up to family members. They often fear rejection. In fact, they may have already felt rejected if family members have spoken negatively about LGBTQ people in the past or made jokes about them. Fortunately, snide comments and jokes about gays are becoming less common. Chances are that they've heard and felt plenty of it while growing up.

Fear of rejection and judgment affects parents too. It can be scary to feel vulnerable by opening up to friends and family, especially Church family. Sometimes fellow Saints feel almost obliged to call out friends on things they feel they're doing wrong. That is seldom helpful and often has the opposite effect. Instead of helping people feel the influence of the Holy Spirit, it can make them defensive as they're buffeted by the spirit of contention. Instead of inspiring people to do better, it can shame them into feeling worse.

In October 2015, Elder Holland related a story in general conference of a family with a gay son. The mention of same-sex attraction over the pulpit made me cry as I immediately thought, "The brethren do get it. They do understand. They do know our families exist."

Elder Holland said, "I speak of a young man who entered the mission field worthily but by his own choice returned home early due to same-sex attraction and some trauma he experienced in that regard. He was still worthy, but his faith was at crisis level, his emotional burden grew ever heavier, and his spiritual pain was more and more profound. He was by turns hurt, confused, angry, and desolate."

This young man's emotional burden and the spiritual pain he felt mirrors so many of the stories people have shared with me since I came out of my own rhetorical closet less than a year before this talk was given.

Elder Holland continued with a phrase that breathed hope into my heart. He said, "And, I must say, this son's sexual orientation did not somehow miraculously change—no one assumed it would. But little by little, his heart changed."[19] As I heard this, I wanted to reach through the television screen and give Elder Holland a huge hug. I thought of the numerous outcries I had received from distraught, hope-seeking LGBTQ individuals who had expressed their sadness and disappointment at not receiving a miraculous change despite their efforts to keep the commandments and serve an honorable mission, along with theirs and other's countless hours of prayer and pleading to God for

19. Jeffrey R. Holland, "Behold Thy Mother," *Ensign*, November 2015.

help and change. I knew those few lines of acknowledgment from an Apostle of God would be healing to many LGBTQ individuals and their parents. Those words would give parents permission to simply love their LGBTQ child with no expectations for change—just love. That kind of love knows no barriers. That kind of love brings people to Christ. Elder Holland's vulnerability and courage to talk about sensitive topics helped fuel my courage and confidence to share my journey and the lessons I have learned through life's experiences.

I have spent a lot of time on my knees, praying for guidance from the Holy Spirit and not my own "natural reactions." As I became more open, honest, and vulnerable, I realized it was improving my relationship with my husband, children, and fellow Saints.

When we decided to tell our extended family about Sean, we felt that sending an email, text, or video link would be the easiest way. We knew we needed to tell our parents in person (my father had already passed away).

Scott told his parents, fully expecting them to have a hard time. He'd heard negative comments about gays while growing up and followed in kind as our kids were growing up. I recalled plenty of times he'd made derogatory comments too. Surprisingly, his folks responded with love and compassion. His mother called Sean at school in Hawaii to make sure he knew how much his grandparents still loved him. That was so important for Sean to hear.

At the time Sean publicly came out, my eighty-two-year-old mother was not in very good health. She was in an assisted living center, and I didn't think she could handle it. She passed away two months later. The day after her passing, I was driving to the mortuary to meet my sisters to make funeral arrangements. I was talking out loud to my mom as if she were sitting next to me in the car. I said, "Mom, now you know all the family secrets such as Sean being gay (and I called out a few other family secrets). Could you please let Sean know how much you love him?"

I ended the conversation by telling my mom how much I was going to miss our weekly visits and daily phone calls, but I hoped it was okay to visit with her in that manner on occasion.

I met up with my sisters at the mortuary. A few hours later, I was back on the road heading home when Sean called. I pulled to the side of the road to talk. Sean told me that earlier he had walked to the neighborhood grocery store and was thinking about "Ma" (that's what he called his grandmother). He said that as he entered the store, the song "Sweet Lorraine" started playing over the store intercom. A ninety-six-year-old man wrote it for his wife, Lorraine. My mother's name is Lorraine. Sean turned and walked back out of the store. He sat down on the curb and cried while sweet memories filled his heart and the love of his grandmother engulfed him.

I asked Sean when all that had happened. He said it had just taken place a few hours earlier. My eyes filled with tears too as I remembered my conversation with my mother a few hours earlier—asking her to please let Sean know how much she loved him. I don't believe in coincidences. Things happen for a reason and with purpose. As I drove home, I thanked Heavenly Father for answered prayers and thanked my mother for letting Sean know that she loved him. I love tender mercies like that. They are a reminder that God is aware of us and truly cares about each one of us.

Faith is so important at such times, because we are reminded that even as parents we are not ultimately in charge of our children's lives—or our own. God watches over all. We must turn our hopes and fears for our children over to Him and trust that He knows His children far better than we do.

As we continued to turn our lives over to God in the best ways we knew how, he continued to use us. I never thought I'd ever be so public about such private matters, but the Lord knew.

Chapter Seven

THE WRESTLE: RECONCILING HARD QUESTIONS

To the individual who is weak in the heart, fearful in the heart, be patient with yourself. Perfection comes not in this life, but in the next life. Don't demand things that are unreasonable, but demand of yourself improvement. As you let the Lord help you through that, He will make the difference.[20]

—President Russell M. Nelson

I'm not a very crafty person, but I do love scrapbooking. One year for Christmas, I decided to make scrapbooks for each of my children. I spent weeks carefully arranging each page with images of childhood while watching old movies. On November 5, 2015, instead of watching movies while scrapbooking, I logged on to the Church's website to listen to past general conference

---

20. Russell M. Nelson, *Men's Hearts Shall Fail Them*; video. See mormon channel.org; accessed July 16, 2019.

talks. At times I felt the spirit so strong that I found myself pausing the talk and taking notes. As I started cleaning up my scrapbooking for the day, Scott called. He was serving as bishop of a Provo young single adult ward at the time and wanted to read me an email he'd received from the stake president earlier that morning. He said he read it four times before he called, thinking he must be missing something. The subject line said, "Revisions to *Handbook 1*." As Scott read the policy regarding same-sex marriages and addressing the children of a parent living in a same-gender relationship, it took me by surprise. I couldn't believe what I was hearing. It read,

A new section in *Handbook 1*, 16.13, will be added as follows:

Children of a Parent Living in a Same-Gender Relationship

A natural or adopted child of a parent living in a same-gender relationship, whether the couple is married or cohabiting, may not receive a name and a blessing.

A natural or adopted child of a parent living in a same-gender relationship, whether the couple is married or cohabiting, may be baptized and confirmed, ordained, or recommended for missionary service only as follows:

A mission president or a stake president may request approval from the Office of the First Presidency to baptize and confirm, ordain, or recommend missionary service for a child of a parent who has lived or is living in a same-gender relationship when he is satisfied by personal interviews that both of the following requirements are met:

1. The child accepts and is committed to live the teachings and doctrine of the Church, and specifically disavows the practice of same-gender cohabitation and marriage.

2. The child is of legal age and does not live with a parent who has lived or currently lives in a same-gender cohabitation relationship or marriage.

This caught me off guard. The LDS Church had recently backed a nondiscrimination bill in Utah that was seeking a balance of religious freedoms and protections against discrimination of LGBTQ people in the workplace and access to housing. Both sides celebrated. When Scott said it was a new Church policy regarding the LGBTQ community, I was expecting to hear words of encouragement toward better inclusion within our congregations. I was taken back and confused. For the first time in my life, I felt my faith shaken.

The new policy indicated for the first time that gay marriage was one of the cases for Church discipline, calling it "apostasy," indicating that the children of gay unions could not receive any ordinances until their eighteenth birthdays, and then, only upon condition of them renouncing same-sex marriage. I thought of all the people I loved in the Latter-day Saint LGBTQ community and how this would likely add more pain to tenuous relationships with the gospel and the Church.

I immediately dropped to my knees and pleaded for understanding from the Lord. As tears trickled down my face, I felt sick. My thoughts clouded over. I knew God loved all His children, but this didn't feel like love.

"Why withhold blessings and opportunities for children because of their parents' choices?" I asked in a somewhat accusatory tone. Yet, almost simultaneously, I heard a voice in my mind reassuring me, "Remember the confirmations of truth you felt today as you listened to general conference." I knew it to be the spirit, which then said to my heart and mind: "Be still. Stay in the boat and love more deeply."

Despite no clarification with regard to the new strict policy change, I rose from my knees with a renewed commitment to love better, stronger, and bolder. I felt the importance of clinging to the truths I did know: Jesus is the Christ, the Son of the living God. The Book of Mormon was translated from ancient golden plates. And I received a confirmation that truths are also taught by modern prophets.

Faith sometimes requires us to follow the prophet before everything makes sense, and sometimes when nothing seems to make any sense at all.

I knew it would be important for me to stretch my arms out further into the LGBTQ community and to others who felt marginalized. Ironically, my husband and I had previously been asked to speak at an Understanding Same Gender Attraction (USGA) meeting in Provo, Utah, later that same day. We had been asked to share our story of embracing the gospel and embracing our gay son with love and inclusion. As Scott and I drove to Provo with a prayer in our heart, our son Sean called to ask if we had heard about the policy that had been leaked and was rapidly being shared on social media. I could hear in his voice that it shook him to the core.

Sean struggled to keep his composure while expressing his shock, hurt, and pain. He said, "Mom I want to marry someday, and I want to have children. I want them to have the opportunity to be baptized and raised in the gospel and advance in the priesthood just like their cousins and friends, if they so choose, without withholding privileges because of my choices." He asked, "Isn't that contrary to the second article of faith?"

Until that day, Sean had been attending church regularly, but now he expressed that he felt the Church didn't want him there. He felt they were drawing a line and there was no place for him. My heart ached. We cried together on the phone. Oh how I wished I could hold him but all I could do was tell him how sorry I was for his pain and how much I loved him. I told him I knew Heavenly Father loved him and all his children. Sean did not doubt my love for him. I prayed he would not doubt God's love for him.

Sean's most immediate concern was the already fragile LGBTQ individuals struggling to reconcile their faith and their sexual orientation. Sean had recently graduated with a master's degree in mental health, and he was afraid this had the potential to increase the suicide statistics. Knowing that many in the LGBTQ community often reached out to me, he said, "Mom, you are going to have a busy night."

The USGA meeting began shortly after we arrived, and Scott and I shared our own personal journey as parents of a gay son with no mention of the newly released policy. Throughout the meeting, people were checking their phones, and it was clear from the looks on their faces that the news of the *Handbook 1* revision was spreading. The second the meeting ended, everyone turned to their neighbor asking if they had heard the news about the new policy. I don't think there was a dry eye in the room. There were lots of hugs, tears, and consoling that night.

I shied away from social media, not knowing what to say and not wanting to be pulled into the angry debate. Two days later, shortly after midnight, I received a text from a friend of another religious faith that said, "Is your family in as much shock as the rest of us? I know you don't get political, but I thought about your situation with your son . . . so just weighing in. Please drop me a line, or if you do a Facebook post, link me to it. I am trying to understand this."

I climbed out of bed and knelt in prayer, asking for the right words to post on Facebook. I wanted something that would touch the hearts of those who were hurting, something that would let people know where I stood. I went to my computer and wrote the following:

> Yes, I am a Mormon. I have a gay son. I love him with all my heart, might, and soul. And I love my religion with all my heart, might, and soul. Things right now are confusing, but just to clarify: I will

never, never turn my back on my son, and I will never, never leave my religious faith. Period. I've been asked how and why. Because God has made it clear to me that I am to love my son unconditionally. I admit it took me awhile to truly understand what the word "unconditionally" meant, because I confused loving to mean condoning, but once I figured out what unconditional really meant, my heart grew a hundredfold for not only my son, but also for people—everyone. As far as my faith goes, it runs deep from a lot of study and prayer and receiving countless confirmations of its truthfulness throughout my life. That I cannot deny. So, for now, I trust, and I will be still for further understanding and move forward loving all the more. I encourage all who read this to reach out in love and kindness to your Latter-day Saint SSA/LGBTQ neighbors, family members, and coworkers who are deeply hurting. There are many—too many—contemplating suicide. Please, please, don't let this be anyone's outcome. Reach out to your LGBTQ neighbors and family members. Give them a hug, invite them to dinner, be a true friend. Show love like your life depended on it, because to them, it does. #sharegoodness

It was around 1:30 a.m. when I finally posted on Facebook. Over the next several days, my post would gather over 1400 likes and over 150 shares. I did not do a follow-up post. I chose to be still and let people process and seek answers for themselves.

Unfortunately, over the next several months, I had many conversations with friends and people in my church congregation who were wrestling with the idea that a couple that had chosen to be married rather than simply live together were now considered apostates. They were especially struggling with the idea that the saving ordinances would be unavailable to the children of same-sex parents until such children reached age eighteen and renounced that marriage. I watched many LGBTQ friends and families who were unable to reconcile their faith and this new policy leave the Church. This pained me, yet I understood where they were coming from.

One positive outcome I could see was that the new policy was bringing many more Saints into an open discussion about how we can minister and care for all of our brothers and sisters. It was heartwarming to read the many stories being shared of neighbors and people from various wards and stakes reaching out with greater compassion and empathy to those who were greatly affected by the policy.

Not long afterward, Sheri Dew gave a talk entitled, "Will You Engage in the Wrestle?" Her talk was followed by her book *Worth the Wrestle*, in which she discusses the mortal challenge of wrestling with questions and with faith. In fact, she wrestled with the same question I had. I was pleasantly surprised to discover that even Sheri Dew had questions.

She describes feelings similar to mine: "When the policy was announced that the children of gay parents might not be eligible for baptism at the traditional age of eight, I was confused. I did not question the Brethren or doubt their inspiration, but neither did I understand the doctrinal basis for the policy. And my heart went out to friends with children or grandchildren in this situation."

She continues, "So I asked the Lord to teach me. I prayed, searched the scriptures, studied the teachings of prophets, and pondered this question in the temple. This went on for months. Then one day a colleague made a statement as part of a presentation that sparked a new thought for me, and in that moment, the Spirit illuminated at least part of the doctrine in my heart and mind. I consider that answer personal revelation and not something I should repeat"[21]

Wrestling with questions can be good. We don't know all the answers. Of course, greater light and knowledge will come, both in this life and in the life to come. Life would be too easy if

---

21. Sheri Dew, *Worth the Wrestle* (Salt Lake City: Deseret Book, 2017), 22–23.

we knew all the answers right now. There would be no need for agency or faith.

The more I have expanded my heart and my mind to truly love and accept our LGBTQ brothers and sisters, the closer I feel to God. I am better able to reconcile each wrestle as I cling to what I know to be true and trust God to give further light and knowledge, whatever that may be, in His time frame not mine.

As unexpected as the first *Handbook 1* policy change came, its reversal, just three and a half years later, was declared on April 4, 2019. It was early in the morning when Scott called me from work with Sean also on the phone. He proceeded to tell us that it had just been announced that the policy regarding LGBT individuals was reversed. Sean asked him if this was a belated April Fool's joke, but Scott assured him it was not. I excitedly said, "Let's hang up the phone so we can get online to see if it is true!" When I was able to verify the news, tears rolled down my cheeks. They were tears of joy and relief. I knelt offering a prayer of gratitude.

The *Church News* released a statement saying,

> At the direction of the First Presidency, President Oaks shared that effective immediately, children of parents who identify themselves as lesbian, gay, bisexual, or transgender may be baptized without First Presidency approval if the custodial parents give permission for the baptism and understand both the doctrine that a baptized child will be taught and the covenants he or she will be expected to make. . . .
>
> Previously, our handbook characterized same-gender marriage by a member as apostasy. While we still consider such a marriage to be a serious transgression, it will not be treated as apostasy for purposes of Church discipline. Instead, the immoral conduct in heterosexual or homosexual relationships will be treated in the same way.
>
> The very positive policies . . . should help affected families. In addition, our members' efforts to show more understanding, compassion, and love should increase respect and understanding among all people of goodwill. We want to reduce the hate and contention so

common today. We are optimistic that a majority of people—whatever their beliefs and orientations—long for better understanding and less contentious communications. That is surely our desire, and we seek the help of our members and others to attain it.

These changes do not represent a shift in Church doctrine related to marriage or the commandments of God in regard to chastity and morality. The doctrine of the plan of salvation and the importance of chastity will not change. These policy changes come after an extended period of counseling with our brethren in the Quorum of the Twelve Apostles and after fervent, united prayer to understand the will of the Lord on these matters.[22]

While I was thrilled about the policy reversal, that happiness was quickly muted by the pain and hurt that Sean and my LGBTQ brothers and sisters were still experiencing and posting on social media. This dramatic shift in policy didn't undo the last three years of pain that many experienced. In fact, it brought it all to the surface again for many people. Their pain is real and valid. Even if I don't feel the pain myself, I don't get to tell them what they should be feeling. I just try to feel what they are feeling with them.

Reversing the earlier policy reflects, to me, a continued wrestling by Church leaders with the many unanswered questions affecting our LGBTQ brothers and sisters. I also feel that this change reflects a unity of the prayers by members of the Church and the Lord's prophets for greater light and knowledge.

As we grow in the gospel, it is natural to have questions and sometimes even doubts. Sincere questions can actually nourish our spiritual growth. My personal experience is that answers to my prayers often come slowly over a period of time. I act upon the

---

22. Dallin H. Oaks, "First Presidency Shares Messages from General Conference Leadership Session," The Church of Jesus Christ of Latter-day Saints Newsroom, April 4, 2019. See newsroom.churchofjesuschrist.org/article/first -presidency-messages-general-conference-leadership-session-april-2019; accessed July 16, 2019.

feelings that are impressed upon my heart and mind, and if I feel peace and comfort, then I know I'm on the right track.

One of the common concerns that parents who reach out to me seem to wrestle with is wondering if they should attend their son or daughter's gay wedding and what message that would send to their other children and grandchildren.

I too have contemplated what message our actions to love and accept Sean in whatever choice he made, including attending his wedding (if that day came) would send to our other children and grandchildren. At the beginning of our journey, I would have said, "No way. That would be condoning, and I do not condone gay marriage. By attending I would be setting a bad example to my grandchildren." I'm apologetic for my strict black and white thinking. I am grateful God has patiently opened my heart and mind to see a better way.

I regret that many of my lessons have come through responding harshly and not from a place of love. I have concluded that Tom Christofferson's mother's response was spot on! If you don't already know their story, let me explain. Tom is Elder Todd D. Christofferon's gay brother.

Scott and I first met Tom in 2014 at a North Star conference (a support group for Latter-day Saint LGBTQ brothers and sisters and their families). I've heard Tom share his story on several occasions. I had recounted his story many times to parents, emphasizing the part of the story where his mother addresses the dilemma of "What message will this send?" Tom's story is now a book entitled, *That We May Be One*. In his own words, Tom describes how his mother responded when he wanted to bring his partner to the family reunion. His brothers with young children were uncomfortable with it to the extent that one family thought they might not bring their children if Tom's boyfriend was present. Sister Christofferon said, "There is no perfect Mormon family. The only thing we can really be perfect at is loving each other."

Then she addressed Tom's brothers and sisters-in-law and said, "The most important lesson your children will learn from how our family treats their Uncle Tom is that nothing they can ever do will take them outside the circle of our family's love."[23] This became their guiding principle. It has become one of ours too.

A particular concern from Latter-day Saint parents and family is illustrated in an email I recently received from a mother of a gay son:

> I am reaching out for guidance and help! I feel sorrow and pain. My struggle is how to reconcile my belief in the gospel while showing 100 percent unconditional love and support for my children. How do I answer the temple recommend question, 'Do you support, affiliate with, or agree with any group or individual whose teachings or practices are contrary to or oppose those accepted by The Church of Jesus Christ of Latter-day Saints?' I feel so torn.

She added, "Why would God command me to love my neighbor and then ask me to turn away from my LGBTQ child?" I feel her pain. I have been asked that question again and again by parents who hold temple recommends, typically after their LGBTQ child has come out as gay, and especially when their child begins dating others of the same sex and/or steps away from the Church. Parents wrestle with how loving and accepting LGBTQ children fits into the temple recommend question and their faith as a whole.

In a press conference on January 27, 2015, Elder Dallin H. Oaks and Elder D. Todd Christofferson were asked the following question regarding Church members who support LGBTQ issues:

> What about Mormons who support same-sex marriage privately among family and friends or publicly by posting entries on Facebook, marching in pride parades, or belonging to gay-friendly

---

23. Christofferson, *That We May Be One*, 19.

organizations such as Affirmation or Mormons Building Bridges? Can they do so without the threat of losing their Church membership or temple privileges?

Elder Christofferson replied,

We have individual members in the Church with a variety of different opinions, beliefs, and positions on these issues and others. . . . In our view, it doesn't really become a problem unless someone is out attacking the Church and its leaders [and in a] deliberate and persistent effort [they are] trying to get others to follow them, trying to draw others away, trying to pull people, if you will, out of the Church or away from its teachings and doctrines.[24]

In a second interview in March 2015, Elder Todd Christofferson also said this:

Reporter: I know that in one of the temple recommend interview questions it asks if you agree with elements that are against the Church and, I guess, I mean, could it be interpreted that if people supported gay marriage that would be agreeing with something that was against the Church?

Christofferson: Well, it's not do you agree with a person's position or an organization's position. It's are you supporting organizations that promote opposition or positions in opposition to the Church.

Reporter: So, would supporting gay marriage threaten somebody's membership in the Church if they went out, say, on Facebook or Twitter, and actively advocated for it?

Christofferson: That's not an organized effort to attack our effort or attack our functioning as a Church, if you will.

Reporter: So members can hold those beliefs even though they're different from what you teach at the pulpit?

Christofferson: Yes. . . . Our approach in all of this, as Joseph Smith said, is persuasion. You can't, he said, use the priesthood and

---

24. Elder Dallin H. Oaks and Elder D. Todd Christofferson, "LDS Leaders Oaks, Christofferson on Religious Freedom, LGBT Rights," January 30, 2015. See archive.sltrib.com/article.php?id=2112602&itype=CMSID; accessed July 16, 2019.

the authority of the Church to dictate. You can't compel, you can't coerce. It has to be gentleness, persuasion, love unfeigned, [like the] words in [the] scripture.[25]

While seeking to reconcile the hard questions, I remind myself to be patient and keep in mind Nephi who was asked if he knew what the condescension of God was. He said, "I know that [God] loveth his children; nevertheless, I do not know the meaning of all things" (I Nephi 11:17). He knew enough. In this life, we will never know the meaning of all things, but we know enough. We know that God loves His children.

Something wonderful happens when we really know, without a doubt, that God loves us. Our questions completely change. Instead of asking, "Why did this happen to me?" or "Why doesn't God care about me?" we say, "Well, I know God loves me, so what can I learn from this experience?"

God already knows what we're made of, but perhaps He wants *us* to learn what we're made of. I think we would all agree that we learn more from our tough times than from our easy times. Sometimes bad things happen to good people. We don't know the meaning of all things, but we know God loves His children! And because He loves us, He will never desert us.[26]

As a disciple of Jesus Christ, I must be willing to believe and accept the truth, even when it is hard to do. One of the most heart-wrenching stories in scripture occurred when "many of [the Lord's] disciples" found it hard to accept His teachings and doctrine, and they "went back, and walked no more with him" (John 6:66).

---

25. See also March 2015 KUTV interview with Elder D. Todd Christofferson, youtube.com/watch?v=XybDk3CEoHg.

26. John Bytheway, "Five Scriptures That Will Help You Get Through Almost Anything," *New Era*, September 2008.

As these disciples left, Jesus turned to the Twelve and asked, "Will ye also go away?" (John 6:67).

Peter responded, "Lord, to whom shall we go? Thou hast the words of eternal life. And we believe and are sure that thou art that Christ, the Son of the living God" (John 6:68–69).

In that moment, when others focused on what they could not accept, the Apostles chose to focus on what they did believe and know, and, as a result, they remained with Christ.[27]

One thing I have come to know is that when we don't fully understand, if we, like Peter, will set aside our fears, our doubts, and our limited understanding and follow Him in faith, things have a way of resolving themselves. An inspired insight or revelation may shed new light on an issue. I remind myself that the Restoration is not an event, but it continues to unfold.

---

27. Elder M. Russell Ballard, "To Whom Shall We Go?" *Ensign*, November 2016.

Chapter Eight

DIFFICULT CONVERSATIONS: NAVIGATING THE LAND MINES OF WHAT TO SAY AND WHAT NOT TO SAY

Unkind things are not usually said under the inspiration of the Lord. The Spirit of the Lord is a spirit of kindness; it is a spirit of patience; it is a spirit of charity and love and forbearance and long suffering.[28]

—*President George Albert Smith*

Parents often tell me they don't know what to say to their LGBTQ child or they are afraid they will say something offensive without knowing, and certainly without meaning to. I still worry sometimes about unintentionally saying something hurtful to Sean, but I have learned that it is so important to not let my fears hold me back from communicating with him. It's so

---

28. *Teachings of Presidents of the Church—George Albert Smith*, "The Power of Kindness," n.p.

very important to keep the lines of communication open and talk beyond the initial coming out conversation, even if it makes you uncomfortable and you don't know what to say.

As I reflect back to my initial conversation with Sean the night he came out to us, and in the months that followed, I remember that I didn't quite know what to say or what not to say, and in my naïveté, I said some pretty hurtful and funny things that weren't meant to be funny or hurtful. I had never researched the subject of LGBTQ, but I found myself giving all kinds of advice anyway. I assumed that Sean came out to his father and me because he wanted us to help *fix* him, so we went into fix-it mode. My initial thought was that boys like girls and girls like boys, therefore perhaps his testosterone levels were out of balance, and if they were at a normal level, he would like girls. So, I ignorantly suggested he see a doctor to have his levels checked. He chuckled, "Mom, it's not testosterone." This conversation made me realize that I had a lot to learn about my son, homosexuality, and God's plan for him, my family, and me.

As Scott and I were raising our seven children, creating a Christ-centered home was important to us. There were times when it became difficult to balance our priorities between school, homework, scouts, sports, piano, dance, and Church callings, along with getting meals, doing the laundry, and washing the dishes. It was difficult, but we did it for each family member so we could create a safe haven for the spirit to dwell. Our expectations included being respectful, cheerful, kind, and considerate of one another and keepers of clean rooms. (I often ignored that last one out of sheer necessity.) We were also mindful of the music our children listened to and the TV programs we watched. While all of our family rules and expectations were coming from a place of love, we were ignorant of the unintentional message some of our rules were sending our children.

For example, Sean recalls us restricting the family from watching *American Idol* when Ellen was asked to be a judge, because she was someone we perceived as pushing the "gay agenda," and we would not support a show that supported her. We also banned the popular talk show *Rosie*, solely because the host was lesbian. I am ashamed that we took no thought that the message we were really sending our children was that LGBTQ individuals were undeserving of our kindness and respect. We had no idea the hurt we were inflicting on Sean as he interpreted our actions to mean he too would be unwelcome in our home if he ever told us he was gay. It literally makes me sick to think of the confusing and hurtful messages our son internalized about himself from the things we said and the rules we set all in the name of "standing for truth and righteousness." In hindsight, we missed out on an opportunity to hold a family council or a family home evening on the subject and to ask our children if they knew anyone at school who identified as LGBTQ. We should have held an open conversation about how to treat our fellow brothers and sisters, regardless of how they look, what they believe, or who they choose to love. In an ideal Mackintosh Christ-centered home, that is what we would have done, but, unfortunately, that was not the reality in our home at that time. We preached charity and kindness, yet we drew lines of intolerance toward those we viewed as choosing to go against God.

My husband Scott knew all the jokes and unkind phrases regarding homosexuality, and he never missed an opportunity to share his view or opinion when a TV show or news report came on that had anything to do with the LGBTQ community. As parents, with self-justification, we could beat ourselves up over the things we have said or done that we wish we had handled differently, but we've come to realize that it serves no one to hold onto grudges or pain. We've learned that being quick to ask for forgiveness and quick to forgive ourselves is key to being able to move forward and become better. Seeking forgiveness from Sean and using the Atonement to forgive ourselves after saying or doing the wrong thing has brought us closer together and closer to the Lord. The Atonement brings healing and peace.

Now, with the words of my mother ringing in my ears, "When you learn a better way, commit to do better," we try each day to press forward in better ways.

I caution parents to not go silent after their son or daughter has come out to them. Most likely your child wants to talk to you openly about what they are feeling. They want you to ask questions, and they need your listening ear to help gain a deeper understanding. One young man told me that after a year of silence following his initial coming-out talk with his mother, he finally brought it up again only to hear her say, "Oh, that's all behind us now. You are over it." This crushed him. His mother had looked at his coming out as a phase, buried it, and moved on with no attempt for further conversations to seek to understand. Please don't be afraid to talk to your loved one if they have opened up to you. Ongoing conversation is so important.

In an effort to help parents avoid the mistakes that I have made, here are several things I have learned to say and do, and to not say and do, as I have navigated difficult conversations:

1. You will never regret listening. You will never regret trying to understand. The Irish proverb by Epictetus says it well: "God gave us two ears and one mouth, so we ought to listen twice as much as we speak."[29] Most LGBTQ individuals share their feelings about attractions only after they have wrestled alone with them and other issues for years. Even if you are the wisest person you know, it is

---

29. Attributed to Epictetus. See Frank N.D. Buchman, "Remaking the World" (London: Blandford Press, 1961), 35.

unlikely that you will know more about the challenges of what they have been experiencing than they do. It is also unlikely that you will learn what they are experiencing without a lot of listening. The most helpful thing a parent can do may be to set the stage for future conversations.

2. Thank your child for trusting you to share this with you. If your child opens up to you, they are showing you that they trust you. It's scary to be vulnerable. Every time someone opens up to another person, they are taking a huge emotional and social risk. They need to know they can trust your confidence—and your calmness—in any situation.[30] Be respectful of their privacy and safe guard their trust by honoring the information they have shared with you. Remember to thank them for having such a firm trust in you. And don't forget that you must continue to be worthy of their trust.

3. You will never regret saying, "I love you." You will never regret throwing your arms around your child and hugging him or her. Express your wholehearted, unconditional love. Also resist the urge to add qualifiers like, "I love you, but . . ." Your child needs to know that they're both loved and lovable. When someone is trying to figure out which direction they want to take their lives, there is something healing, liberating, and empowering about knowing that your love is not conditional upon them making certain choices. The words "I love you and respect you even more for sharing" are powerful. Physical expressions of that love and affection, such as a meaningful hug, can also go a long way.

---

30. The Church of Ziontology, "How to Be a Better Parent."

4. Avoid preaching, lecturing, or unhelpful and hurtful phrases such as "We all have our challenges." "If you had more faith, you could overcome same-sex attraction, get married, etc." "If you would only apply the Atonement of Christ in your life." These kinds of phrases are *not* helpful. It's important to understand that God works in our individual lives in very different ways. Sometimes life experiences are divinely committed tutorials that will teach individuals certain things that God wants them to learn. Rather than attributing your child's sexual orientation or gender identity to a trial, a lack of faith, or his or her understanding of the Atonement, you can offer the most support simply by listening, loving, and inspiring by example.

5. Keep the lines of communication open. Pause and ask yourself if your words and actions are going to keep the line of communication open with your LGBTQ loved one or if they will create a wedge and distance in your relationship. Stopping to ask myself that simple question before I react has served our relationship well. When I approach difficult conversations with my son—or really anyone—I focus on coming from a place of empathy and love. The words attributed to Carl W. Buehner come to mind: "They may forget what you said—but they will never forget how you made them feel."[31] Your open heart and kindness will have an effect on your LGBTQ loved one. At the end of the day, that's what they will remember. They will want to reciprocate your kindness and the doors of communication will naturally open. Taped to my bedroom mirror where I can see it every day is the old Hindi word *Genshai,*

---

31. Attributed to Carl W. Buehner. See *Richard Evans' Quote Book* (Publisher's Press, 1971), n.p.

which means, "Never treat a person in a manner that would make them feel small."[32] This has become my foundation in approaching conversations of all types.

6. Resist any impulse to give counsel unless it's being requested. Simply be willing to love and listen first. It's not your responsibility to have all the answers. You don't need all or even any answers to questions in order to be a support. Put the ball in your child's court and ask them how they need you to support them. Ask questions like, "What has this been like for you?" "What's the hardest part?" or "How can I best support you?"

7. Don't say, "Of course. I've suspected all along." More often than not, your child has spent a good amount of time and energy trying to blend in and act in such a way that others won't have suspected, so a comment like this could make them feel overwhelmingly vulnerable. Although you may think that you're being supportive by telling your child that you already knew about their sexuality, it's typically best to respond as if you had no idea and let them lead the conversation from there.

8. Don't use the terms "suffering from" or "struggling with" same-sex attraction or gender-dysphoria. While some individuals may indeed experience struggle or suffering as they seek to understand their feelings, or experience deep pain because of abuse, bullying, or loneliness, LGBTQ isn't a disease. It is not contagious. Your son or daughter may prefer to use the term gay as opposed to saying

---

32. Kevin Hall, *Aspire: Discovering Your Purpose through the Power of Words* (Riverton, UT: Bookwise Publishing, 2009), 9.

they are experiencing same-sex attraction. My practice is to reflect back the terminology they find most meaningful to them in describing their experience or identity. If you are unsure, ask them what they prefer you use.

9. Avoid making assumptions about the path your child will or should take. Instead, ask, "So what are your plans?" Agency is one of the most fundamental principles of the gospel, and while the gospel principal is clear regarding sexual behavior, the greatest power comes from choosing to live those laws from a place of internal desire rather than external pressure. Simply asking questions from a place of genuine care and interest is the most empowering support you can offer. Make sure they feel that they have space to explore what it is they want for themselves without pressuring or shaming them into choosing one direction or another. Put aside preconceived ideas, judgments, or opinions about LGBTQ and simply spend time with them and listen. Don't confine yourself to thinking only in terms of how you believe your child should respond to their feelings. Seek to understand their dreams, motivations, and desires instead. Be careful not to assume you know the person better than they know themselves or what the best choice for their life might be.

10. Avoid comparison. "Hey, I read this story about someone who is gay and is happily married to someone of the opposite sex. Have you thought about pursuing a heterosexual marriage?" Many LGBTQ individuals have happy and fulfilling heterosexual marriages, but many of these marriages end in divorce. Pursuing a heterosexual marriage is a personal decision. It's something each person has to work out with the Lord on his or her own. Many

people may not marry in this life, and it can be discouraging and isolating to frequently hear either the question of why they're not married or comments about singleness that leave anyone who is alone in the Church feeling as if they're failing at mortality. No one wants to be continually compared to others or implicitly reminded of how someone else's lot in life is perceivably better. Having a variety of examples to look to can be very helpful, but when those examples are imposed on someone, it can be more discouraging than anything. Sometimes family and friends falsely believe that their loved ones would be freed of their same-sex attraction if they would just get married. This not helpful, and Church leaders have specifically counseled against recommending marriage as a means of reducing same-sex attraction. In the October 2007 general conference, Elder Jeffrey R. Holland said, "Recognize that marriage is not an all-purpose solution. Same-gender attractions run deep, and trying to force a heterosexual relationship is not likely to change them. We are all thrilled when some who struggle with these feelings are able to marry, raise children, and achieve family happiness. But other attempts have resulted in broken hearts and broken homes."[33]

As a parent, I believe we are in a unique position to ask questions, request specifics, and inquire about our children's feelings and opinions. As you turn to the Lord, He will guide you, for He has said, "And now, verily, verily, I say unto thee, put your trust in that Spirit which leadeth to do good—yea, to do justly, to walk humbly, to judge righteously; and this is my Spirit"

---

33. Jeffrey R. Holland, "Helping Those Who Struggle with Same-Gender Attraction," *Ensign*, October 2007.

(D&C 11:12). I know that when I look up to heaven, the Spirit prepares my heart and mind, and He will prepare yours as well. You will also find that the Lord puts other helpers by your side— on your right, on your left, and all around you.[34]

Difficult conversations don't need to be difficult or scary. They can be a meaningful and loving experience between you and your LGBTQ child.

34. Henry B. Eyring, "Trust in That Spirit Which Leadeth to Do Good," *Ensign*, May 2016.

Chapter Nine

FEELING JUDGED VS. FEELING LOVED

During that final evening with my sister, I believe God was asking me, "Can't you see that everyone around you is a sacred being?"[35]

—*Elder Robert C. Gay*

Early one Sunday morning, Sean called to ask if he and his boyfriend could come to church with us. It caught me off guard. I knew he hadn't been to church in a very long time, so I excitedly said, "Yes!"

Then I was overcome with fear as I thought of how my son and his boyfriend might be judged. "What will people think?" That thought came through so forcefully I was afraid I'd said it out loud. Fortunately, I had not.

---

35. Robert C. Gay, "Taking upon Ourselves the Name of Jesus Christ," *Ensign*, November 2018.

I'm not sure why I was so afraid. Sean had grown up in this ward. He'd served as president of the deacons' and teachers' quorums as well as first assistant to the bishop in the priests' quorum. He had delivered his missionary homecoming report here. Ward members had shown kindness to my youngest daughter who did not fit the Latter-day Saint mold either. She had a nose ring, gauges, and was expecting a baby out of wedlock.

Would they extend that same kindness to our son? Would they slide over and make room for us on the pew? Would they stare and whisper when the sacrament bread and water was passed without them partaking? I was fine if those actions were directed at me, but the protective mother in me didn't want those actions directed toward my children. More than anything, I wanted my children to feel welcomed and loved.

As I walked into the chapel with my pregnant daughter, *and* my gay son, *and* his boyfriend, I watched for awkward stares but saw none. The people who *did* look our way smiled and nodded. I slowly breathed a sigh of relief. Finally, I could feel my body relax as some of the anxiety left. I reminded myself that I was among friends.

I was also extended a tender mercy when the opening song was one of my favorites: "Because I Have Been Given Much." As I sat there with one arm around my unwed, pregnant daughter and my other arm around my gay son, gratitude filled my heart, and the tears began to flow. Two of my children were with me at church and had come of their own accord. I had a wonderful husband; seven grown children, four of which were married and raising children of their own; and a son on a mission.

Through experiences I've had with my children, I have learned that even when we disagree we can still be respectful of our differences and find plenty to love in one another. They taught me lessons in love that I don't think I could have learned any other way. I was grateful that my son and daughter had the courage to come to church with me. And I was so grateful to my Church family who showed kindness and acceptance. It was a much-welcomed tender mercy.

Following the Church meeting, my daughter received a genuine hug from her visiting teacher. Many in the congregation shook my son's hand and introduced themselves to his companion. My heart filled with deep gratitude as I witnessed true Christlike love.

I ponder often on that day—it's one of my fondest memories. It's easy to go to church when you feel everything is on track and going well, but it can be a real struggle if you feel your life and faith don't fit with the culture or your life doesn't align with the standards everyone else seems to uphold. I am deeply grateful for the loving response of our ward to my son and his companion and to my daughter. I have thanked my bishop on numerous occasions for the loving and welcoming reception we received that day.

In the October 2018 general conference, Elder Robert C. Gay tells a touching story about visiting his sister the evening of her passing. She'd had a challenging life, struggled with the gospel, and was never really active. He said,

> I gave her a blessing to peacefully return home. At that moment, I realized I had too often defined my sister's life in terms of her trials and inactivity. As I placed my hands on her head that evening, I received a severe rebuke from the Spirit. I was made acutely aware of her goodness and allowed to see her as God saw her—not as someone who struggled with the gospel and life but as someone who had to deal with difficult issues I did not have. I saw her as a magnificent mother who, despite great obstacles, had raised four beautiful, amazing children. I saw her as the friend to our mother who took time to watch over and be a companion to her after our father passed away.[36]

---

36. Gay, "Taking upon Ourselves the Name of Jesus Christ."

When speaking of the importance of casting away judgment and loving each person who walks through the chapel doors, Sister Carol F. McConkie taught,

> I know people who come to church every Sunday so they can be inspired and uplifted and who just simply walk away feeling judged, unloved, and unneeded—like there is no place for them in the Church.
>
> We need to do this differently. We need to be deeply aware of what the purpose of coming to church on Sunday is and make sure that everyone who comes feels loved, needed, accepted, and lifted. Everybody has struggles we don't even know about. It's so important that we be aware that everyone around us is loved of God and that we need to see them through Christlike eyes. We cannot allow judgment to dictate the way we interact with people. It's just simply not right.
>
> I feel that the Lord places us where we are and connects us with the people around us for a purpose, because it is not only about our own progression but also about helping others progress. I've come to recognize that we are placed where we are so that we can love and lift others.
>
> We just cannot be or even call ourselves a disciple of Christ if we are not helping others along that path. The gospel of Jesus Christ does not marginalize people; people marginalize people, and we have to fix that. We need to be sensitive, and love them and allow them the opportunity to grow and to blossom and to be their best selves. They have talents and abilities and personalit[ies] that are needed in the kingdom of God.
>
> And if we are going to build the Kingdom of God on the earth, we need everyone to come—to come and do their part—and we need to recognize that. When anyone's shadow darkens the door of a chapel, they ought to feel immediately embraced and loved and lifted and inspired.[37]

---

37. Carol F. McConkie, "Lifting Others"; video or transcript. See churchof jesuschrist.org/media-library or ldsliving.com, November 2, 2016; both accessed July 17, 2019.

I've learned the importance of casting aside judgment in search of understanding and compassion. I have worked harder at coming from a place of love and empathy. I have learned that if I focus on the positive and approach difficult situations from a place of love, I can see more beauty and less disaster.

One day I called Sean to see if his father and I could come see the progress on the home he and his partner had purchased. As we compared our schedules, it looked like the best day would be Monday evening. I said, "Perfect! We'll come for family home evening. I'll bring dinner and a lesson." Sean chuckled and said, "Okay, sounds good." When Monday rolled around, Sean called to ask, "Are you still coming for family 'homo' evening?"

This time I chuckled and replied, "Yes, we will see you at 6:00!" We brought dinner, but I didn't bring a prepared lesson. Instead, we helped him and his partner with some fix-it projects and spent time just visiting. When it was time to head back home, I said, "Before we leave, can we kneel and end in prayer?"

The four of us knelt together and Sean offered a beautiful prayer. In our home after family prayers, we stand and hug each person individually, and this night was the same. Scott and I hugged Sean, and we hugged his partner. As we drove home, we talked about how wonderful it is to have a close relationship with Sean and that we can kneel in prayer together. To me, family success is about relationships, spending time together, and creating memories. It hasn't been an easy road, and we are far from perfect, but I try my best to remember that God's job is to judge and my job is to love.

Scott and I are learning over time how to hold to the values and standards of the gospel while being inclusive of all our children. We seek to maintain the spirit as best we can, most especially the spirit of love.

In the Sermon on the Mount, Jesus said, "Judge not, that ye be not judged." This may sound like a warning or a restriction, but instead I see it as an exciting promise. He continues, "For with what judgment ye judge, ye shall be judged: and with what measure ye mete, it shall be measured to you again" (Matthew 7:1–2). What is Christ promising us here? He is saying that the measure, or judgment, we dole out will be measured to us again—that we will receive whatever we measure out. So, what if we measure out what Christ would? What is his measure?

His measure is all that measure in abundance: filled up, shaken together, pressed down, and running over. If we measure out what Christ would, if we are generous, tolerant, accepting, and loving, that's exactly how we will be treated.[38]

I don't know if my son and daughter will ever be at church every Sunday. Maybe another child will decide that church isn't for them anymore. Maybe my son will never get married in the temple. But I can live with it, because I trust God. I trust in His promises. I trust that He loves me, He loves my children, and He blessed me with the children that I have for a reason.

Taped to my bathroom mirror are two words: love and trust. Love is to remind me to do just that—love. Trust is a reminder to trust in the Lord, trust in the journey, trust in the process, trust in *His* plan.

---

38. Okazaki, *What a Friend We Have in Jesus*, 98.

Chapter Ten

CHARITY, THE PURE LOVE OF CHRIST

Love is one of the chief characteristics of Deity . . . A man [or woman] filled with the love of God, is not content with blessing his [or her] own family alone, but ranges through the whole world, anxious to bless the whole human race.[39]

—*Prophet Joseph Smith*

I distinctly remember the first time I knelt by my bed and prayed to ask God, "Are you there? Do you really love me?" I was only ten years old. Still, it had become very important for me to find out if God really *did* know me and if I really *did* matter to Him.

Right after I asked Heavenly Father if He loved me, it felt like He wrapped His arms around me and held me close. I have never forgotten that feeling and that answer to my prayer. I still hold that memory close to this day. It formed the foundation of

---

39. Joseph Smith, *Teachings of the Prophet Joseph Smith*, sel. Joseph Fielding Smith (Salt Lake City: Deseret Book, 1938), 174.

my testimony that God is real and He loves me. And if God loves me, then I know He loves all His children.

I believe that one of the most powerful ways we can gain more charity is by having an increased personal awareness—through the Holy Ghost—of how much our Father in Heaven and Savior love us. As that love fills our own hearts, our capacity to receive and to give love expands to overflowing. Our immediate response upon tasting of the fruit of the tree of life, the pure love of God, can be like that of our father Lehi:

"And as I partook of the fruit thereof it filled my soul with exceedingly great joy; wherefore, I began to be desirous that my family should partake of it also; for I knew that it was desirable above all other fruit" (1 Nephi 8:12).

The Apostle Paul and the prophet Mormon both say that charity is the pure love of Christ, for which we should fervently pray with all "energy of heart." Nothing else counts if love is lacking.

Charity enables us to speak the language of angels. We can have the gift of prophecy. We can possess all knowledge and have faith so great we can move mountains. We can give away everything we possess and even become martyrs for our faith, but without love, we are no more than the sound of a bell or cymbal that attracts attention for a few seconds but then dies away on the air. (See 1 Corinthians 13:1–3 and Moroni 7:44–48.)

I've learned the importance of exercising my agency and choosing to continue in charity and prayer as best as I can, asking God to do His work of love in me and to help me feel and express that love to others.

I am grateful beyond measure for the ways in which the Lord blesses, teaches, and supports us—in good times and in bad. He journeys with us through our adversity while honoring our agency and the agency of our loved ones.

We are all a work in progress, and that's okay. In fact, that is how it is intended to be. My friend Kimberly Giles taught me that life is a classroom, and mistakes don't count against our final grade. We're still in the learning stages. Making a mistake means we can try again, without fear of failure, ridicule, or shame. In a classroom, mistakes mark course corrections and further education, not punishment. By thinking in terms of life being a classroom, I'm better able to look at every experience, every conversation, and every encounter with others (especially my son) as an opportunity to learn and love.[40]

In the fall of 2016, the Church rolled out an updated and more interactive Mormon and Gay website containing firsthand accounts of Church members who experience same-sex attraction or identify as gay, lesbian, or bisexual. I was happy to see that the website had changed its name from Mormons and Gays, which sounded like an "us" verses "them," to the more inclusive name Mormon and Gay, which seemed to acknowledge one could be Mormon *and* Gay. I couldn't have imagined in a million years that the Church would reach out to us and ask us to share our story on their updated website.

We were flattered that the Church would want to include our story, and nervous about doing it. It was different from the other stories on the website, because they featured stories of lesbian, gay, and bisexual individuals choosing to live within the framework of the gospel and who were not currently in same-sex relationships. We were the parents of a gay son who was currently dating another young man. They said they wanted our family's story for that reason—because so many families are navigating a similar journey. We could provide an added perspective that could help others.

---

40. Kimberly Giles, *Choosing Clarity: The Path to Fearlessness* (Thomas Noble Books, 2014), 81.

Charity. That's what it boiled down to. Were we willing to be vulnerable in sharing our story, simply in the hope of helping others, or at least one other soul? Absolutely. We personally knew many families who yearned for a story to be shared on the Mormon and Gay website that addressed some of the challenges of having a child come out as LGBT and step away from the Church.

First we got the approval from Sean and our other children, including Sean's boyfriend at the time. The Church website spokesman said they wanted everyone to be included in the video since we included everyone in our family gatherings.

Sean was understandably hesitant to say yes. He was afraid he'd be used as the bad example—what *not* to do. We were assured that the theme of the video would be love and inclusion (which proved to be very much the case). Still, like us, Sean was interested in helping others who could use help.

The film crew spent two days in our home. They interviewed me, Scott, and Sean. They filmed our entire family eating dinner and playing together on the front lawn. One year later, on March 17, 2017, the six-minute video of our family and our written articles were added to the Church's official Mormon and Gay website.

It was definitely unnerving to be so vulnerable and open. However, that sacrifice has already paid off in large dividends. It has been a marvelous experience to hear from people around the world. Many have reached out to thank us for helping them navigate similar family situations. Most are doing all they can, which is all the Lord expects from us. He does the rest, which is so much more.

In a *Deseret News* article interview, Sean was quoted as saying that the greatest blessing in his life is the fact that his family is always there for him. He said, "I know many individuals . . . [who] come out to [their families] and their families no longer talk to them. They were kicked out of their homes [and] are no longer going to family dinners or family events. It's scary that that could have so easily happened to me, but it didn't. My family loved and recognized me for who I was. It wasn't immediate, but it's something that took place. I know my family always has my back and that they're there for me and love me."

I know my courage to share comes from turning to God for strength to do so. Such strength has often come in the form of charity. Through trying to help others, we've been tested, tried, and blessed with the cleansing effects of ministering as the Savior would have us minister.

I don't say any of that to downplay the pain, the shock, or whatever else this may entail. Just when I think I have it all figured out, something else shifts—usually in a big way!

The latest endeavor occurred in the spring of 2019. Sean told me he was going to propose to his boyfriend Karson of two and a half years. I asked him, "How do you know he's not planning to ask you? Who decides that?"

He laughed and said that Karson had always told him that he needed to be the one to propose. "Do you have a ring? Wait! Do you give each other engagement rings?" I never had to ask my other six children these questions. This was new territory.

He said, "Yes, I have a ring." He told me he was nervous, because he was meeting with his potential in-laws that evening to let them know of his plans and to ask for their blessing. I was glad he felt it important to talk to the parents and ask for their blessing. He sent me a late-night text that read, "The talk went well!"

Sean's friends from school were all married with children. He had watched his six siblings get married. Now it was finally his turn.

I realized how far I'd come in accepting our reality. Just a few years earlier I would have cried until there were no more tears. Now I am finding happiness for his happiness.

After Sean proposed, he called his father and me to tell us his boyfriend said yes. We congratulated him and asked for the details of how he proposed. Then he sent a group text to his siblings and their spouses. The thread went on and on with congratulations. The following day, he announced his engagement publicly on Facebook, which included engagement photos. I was at a gas station, leaning against my car, checking my Facebook feed as I waited for the tank to fill.

I sat down in the car and shut the door as a moment of grief rolled over me. At first I had no idea why I would feel sad. I was truly happy that he was happy and that he was marrying someone he loved that loved him. Yet, I felt a deep ache as I acknowledged my son was marrying another man and would not be marrying a woman in the temple—the dream I seemed to be holding on to, as parents are known to do for their children.

My mind raced back to a conversation I had with Sean two days after same-sex marriage became legal in the state of Utah (October 6, 2014).[41] He sent me a text that said, "Mom you hurt my feelings!" This did not sound like a conversation to have via text, so I immediately called him and asked what I had unknowingly done to hurt him.

He said, "Mom, it's legal for same-sex couples to get married in Utah."

I said, "Yes, I know."

He went on to say, "That announcement was huge for me. It was one of the best days of my life, and not you or dad reached out to congratulate me."

---

41. Dennis Romboy, "Same-sex marriage now legal in Utah," *Deseret News*, October 6, 2014. See deseretnews.com/article/865612522/Same-sex-marriage-stay-lifted-in-Utah-marriage-licenses-issued-in-Salt-Lake-City.html; accessed August 19, 2019.

His disappointment rang clear. I was sad that I had unintentionally hurt Sean, but I answered in all honesty, "I'm sorry, but congratulations didn't even cross my mind."

He said, "Mom, you know I want to get married someday, and I want my family to be there. Now that it's legal in Utah, it could really happen. I don't want my wedding to feel like a funeral. I want people to be happy for me."

Together we cried. My son's grief and the conflict between my love for him and my faith in God's command that marriage be between a man and a woman was breaking my heart. And I knew my son's heart was also breaking at the thought that I may not support him on his special day. This was something I didn't take lightly. I didn't want Sean to live a life alone, and though the thought of him marrying a man was not something I ever envisioned in his future, I knew and still know that agency is an essential element of God's plan. I knew my job as a parent was to just love him the best I could and trust in the Lord for the rest.

I allowed myself to feel sorrow, and then I laid it at my Savior's feet. I am grateful that the Lord teaches me with each act of mourning that He loves me and He loves my son. Agency is an essential element of God's plan, and charity never faileth.

We moved forward making wedding plans and offered Sean our help in the planning and whatever he needed. One of the Mackintosh family traditions is to throw a wedding shower for the engaged couple (organized by the aunts) that includes the brothers, sisters, aunts, uncles, grandparents, and cousins of both families. It was a tradition started to bring the families of the soon-to-be-married couple together to meet one another before the busy wedding day. This would be the first shower thrown for a same-sex couple, and I hoped that the families of Sean and Karson would display the same level of zeal and participation as they did for other cousin wedding showers.

The day of the shower party, the invited guests showed up by the carloads. Over seventy family members attended. It was a lovely evening as we got to know each other's families and see and feel the love for Sean and Karson. It was charity at its finest.

The week of the wedding, my married children living out of state flew in. One son-in-law, who didn't think it was possible for him to attend, booked a flight at the last minute. It would be the first time in four years that all seven of my children and their spouses would be together. That alone was something to celebrate. My house was full, and my heart was bursting to have all my children together, even if their schedules only permitted them to stay a couple of days. They all knew it meant the world to Sean for them to be there.

The wedding ceremony took place in the mountains, surrounded by brothers, sisters, aunts, uncles, grandparents, and many friends. Sean's sisters and sisters-in-law, along with Karson's sister-in-law, were bridesmaids, each dressed in white lace dresses. The brothers and brothers-in-law were groomsmen, dressed in white shirts and gray pants with brown suspenders.

As I looked over the crowd of attendees, I knew many had attended in full support of Sean and Karson's commitment to one another in marriage, while others were feeling uncomfortable. Nevertheless, they all showed up. It had nothing to do with political or moral views and everything to do with being there as family and friends. It was a day without overtones of a funeral. There was a feeling of closeness and strengthened family bonds. It was a day of kindness, respect, joy, and love. All who attended added to the emotional safety, security, and fond memories. It will be a day for Sean and Karson to always remember and reflect upon. Charity never faileth.

As a parent, and as a Latter-day Saint, I am asked to seek after charity and show it toward all—especially my own children. My job is to love them and trust in the Lord to do the rest.

The words of Susan Evans McCloud say it well:

Savior, may I learn to love thee,
Walk the path that thou hast shown,
Pause to help and lift another,
Finding strength beyond my own. . . .

Who am I to judge another
When I walk imperfectly?
In the quiet heart is hidden
Sorrow that the eye can't see. . . .

I would be my brother's keeper;
I would learn the healer's art.
To the wounded and the weary
I would show a gentle heart.

I would be my brother's keeper—
Lord, I would follow thee.[42]

---

42. "Lord, I Would Follow Thee," *Hymns*, no. 220.

Chapter Eleven

PEACE AND PERSPECTIVE

When the Holy Ghost assures heart and mind of truth, darkness and doubt flee.[43]

"Mom, Dad, I'm gay."

When I first heard those words from our son and felt the impact of such a declaration, I never imagined I would find joy in the journey that lay ahead. Yet, that is precisely what has happened. I no longer see having a gay child as a challenge. I see it as a blessing to learn and grow together.

I married Scott Mackintosh in the Salt Lake Temple on September 22, 1983. I had grand expectations and very high hopes. I was certain that if we attended church, studied the scriptures, prayed individually and as a family, held family home evenings, paid our tithing, and loved and served one another, then joy would flow into our lives without a hitch.

---

43. "The Visiting Teacher: Seeking Knowledge and a Witness of Truth," *Ensign*, October 1999.

We taught our children the principles of the gospel. We knelt in family prayer. We attended sporting events, camping trips, scouts, and pinewood derbies (which can challenge anyone's faith). We were confident in our labors that each son and daughter would grow up with the same depth of testimony and the same level of commitment to God and His restored gospel that Scott and I had. However, the reality is that no matter how hard we try and how often we do our best, life seldom goes as planned. Each of God's children has his or her own agency. We all come to earth as individual and unique spirits. Upon receiving a mortal body, we are affected in different ways by different combinations of nature and nurture. Not only does that make it impossible for us to predict how each of our lives will unfold, but it's also why the Lord has commanded us that we should "judge not unrighteously . . . but judge righteous judgment" (Joseph Smith Translation, Matthew 7:2; see also John 7:24 and Alma 41:14).

I may not understand all of God's plan for me and my family. I may not know why many of God's children are LGBTQ. Yet, I have learned to trust that my Heavenly Parents know. They know the challenges and opportunities each of us needs to learn, grow, and stretch as we become more like Him.

I've discovered that no matter what our individual circumstances may be, we can receive a witness of the Spirit as we seek it—whether we are navigating another bump in the road, gaining a testimony, strengthening the testimony we already have, seeking help and comfort with a difficult problem or decision, or looking for ways to strengthen our families. The Lord Himself has promised, "I will impart unto you of my Spirit, which shall enlighten your mind, which shall fill your soul with joy" (D&C 11:13).

As members of The Church of Jesus Christ of Latter-day Saints, we are asked to "Seek ye diligently and teach one another words of wisdom; yea, seek ye out of the best books words of wisdom; seek learning, even by study and also by faith" (D&C 88:118).

As a parent of an LGBTQ child, I am strongly affected by that verse. This has been a journey of seeking answers, exercising faith, learning, stretching, growing, exercising more faith, and trusting that through the enabling power of grace, God will handle the rest—before, during, and after all I can do. (See "Grace" in the Bible dictionary and 2 Nephi 25:23.)

At a BYU Question and Answer devotional, Elder M. Russell Ballard said,

> My calling and life experiences allow me to respond to certain types of questions. There are other types of questions that require an expert in a specific subject matter. This is exactly what I do when I need an answer to such questions: I seek help from others, including those with degrees and expertise in such fields.
>
> I worry sometimes that members expect too much from Church leaders and teachers—expecting them to be experts in subjects well beyond their duties and responsibilities. The Lord called the apostles and prophets to invite others to come unto Christ—not to obtain advanced degrees in ancient history, biblical studies, and other fields that may be useful in answering all the questions we may have about scriptures, history, and the Church. Our primary duty is to build up the Church, teach the doctrine of Christ, and help those in need of help.
>
> Fortunately, the Lord provided this counsel for those asking questions: If you have a question that requires an expert, please take the time to find a thoughtful and qualified expert to help you.[44]

---

44. M. Russell Ballard, "Questions and Answers," BYU Devotional, Nov. 14, 2017. (See speeches.byu.edu.; accessed July 17, 2019.)

The mormonandgay.churchofjesuschrist.org website contains important insights, including,

> Seek knowledge, and learn all you can. Speak with your bishop or branch president and receive counsel from an authorized servant of the Lord. If you feel impressed, ask him for a priesthood blessing to help you meet the needs of your child. Some people find perspective in support groups or through temple attendance. In fact, there is no better place to find peace and perspective than in the temple.[45]

After our son Sean came out to us, I quickly discovered I knew very little about LGBTQ. I went on a "seek knowledge and learn all you can" frenzy. I searched the scriptures, Church talks and books, and talked to others on a similar journey. What I have found to be most helpful is turning to God for guidance and direction. By turning to the Savior, I have found peace. I feel Him near. I can feel His love for my family and me. He knows far better than I what my son needs. Honestly, I don't know how people do this "mortal life thing" without Him.

Frequent temple attendance helps me focus on the promises made between God and myself. I am better able to view life from an eternal perspective. In addition, as the Mormon and gay website states, "Some people find perspective in support groups." I am one of those people. I take part in online (and land) support groups for Latter-day Saint parents of LGBTQ. This has given me the opportunity to not only receive support, but also to extend support to others. It's nice to be able to talk to other parents navigating a similar path. My husband and I host quarterly parent support meetings in our home so parents can share openly in a safe space, offering and receiving strength from each other and

---

45. "Ten Tips for Parents." See mormonandgay.churchofjesuschrist.org; accessed July 17, 2019.

the Lord. "For where two or three are gathered together in [the Lord's] name," He is in our midst. (See Matthew 18:20.)

North Star and Affirmation are the two support groups I am most familiar with. While both groups are supportive of Latter-day Saint LGBTQ individuals, they differ somewhat, and I tend to recommend one or the other—or both—depending on each person's situation. Their websites provide information that can be helpful in making such choices.

For instance, North Star is "a faith-affirming resource for Latter-day Saints addressing sexual orientation and gender identity, and who desire to live in harmony with the teachings of Jesus Christ and the doctrines and values of The Church of Jesus Christ of Latter-day Saints" (northstarlds.org).

Affirmation fosters "intersectional awareness, inclusivity (regardless of location on the faith spectrum), healing, self-acceptance, and spiritual self-reliance of LGBT Mormons, both in and out of the LDS Church" (affirmation.org/who-we-are/our-vision/). They also "avoid taking positions on Church doctrine."

The Church cannot and does not endorse these or any other support groups. It takes the position that "some people find perspective in support groups" (mormonandgay.churchofjesuschrist.org). Reaching out to other parents and individuals can be helpful. Being prayerful and leaning on the Spirit can provide guidance as to where to turn for support.

Unfortunately, while we as parents are seeking peace and perspective, Satan is focused on wreaking havoc on our souls and the souls of our sons and daughters. He wants all of us to be miserable like he is, and he'll stop at nothing to destroy individuals and families. Fortunately, the Lord has supreme power.

Paul tells us that "we have no might against this great company that cometh against us; neither know we what to do: but our eyes are upon thee. . . . Thus saith the Lord unto you, Be not afraid nor dismayed by reason of this great multitude; for the battle is not yours, but God's" (2 Chronicles 20:12, 15).

The Lord offers us great confidence through His prophet Elisha. "Fear not: for they that be with us are more than they that be with them" (2 Kings 6:16). And He promises us, "I will be on your right hand and on your left, and my Spirit shall be in your hearts, and mine angels round about you, to bear you up" (D&C 84:88).

Elder Jeffrey R. Holland provides hope too. He said,

> I ask everyone within the sound of my voice to take heart, be filled with faith, and remember the Lord has said He would 'fight [our] battles, [our] children's battles, and [the battles of our] children's children' (D&C 98:37). And what do we do to merit such a defense? We are to 'search diligently, pray always, and be believing [then] all things shall work together for [our] good, if [we] walk uprightly and remember the covenant wherewith [we] have covenanted' (D&C 90:24).
>
> The latter days are not a time to fear and tremble. They are a time to be believing and remember our covenants.[46]

This journey can seem overwhelming at times. Still, I testify that we have a loving and all-powerful Heavenly Father who is at the lead in our battles, and it is so important for us to stay with Him. After all, we know who wins in the end—He who has already conquered death after suffering our "pains and afflictions and temptations of every kind; and this that the word might be fulfilled which saith he will take upon him the pains and the sicknesses of his people" (Alma 7:11).

Our challenge is to allow the Savior to lead us and to give Him the things that we are hanging onto that weigh us down. He

---

46. Elder Jeffrey R. Holland, "The Ministry of Angels," *Ensign*, November 2008.

will make our burdens light and give us joy in our journey. I have found peace as I embrace our unique positions in our journeys back home. I testify of the peace He has brought into our lives.

"Peace I leave with you, my peace I give unto you: not as the world giveth, give I unto you. Let not your heart be troubled, neither let it be afraid" (John 14:27).

BECOMING THE PARENT
MY CHILD NEEDS

By Scott Mackintosh

M y son Sean came home from college on Christmas break a few years ago and sent my wife and me a message that changed all our lives: "Hey, I'm not going to beat around the bush too much. I'm just going to tell you something that I'm sure you already know or that has at least crossed your mind at times. I'm gay . . ."

I thought, *No, I didn't know that, and I didn't think it either. Why would I ever think that?*

The fact that he came out and told us in a message on Facebook was mind-boggling at first. But looking back, that was one of the best things he could have done. It gave me time to cool down and sift through the many thoughts that were whirling around in my head. I immediately asked Becky if she'd gotten the same message. She had. I was consumed with anger, and in my shock and anger, I said some really mean things. I'm glad Becky was the only one who heard them. I couldn't figure out why Sean would choose to be gay, because, at the time, I mistakenly believed that people chose it.

By the time Sean got back to our house that night, I had already gone to bed. Fortunately, Becky was awake and talked with him until four o'clock in the morning. Afterward, she came back into the room, and I asked where she had been. She said she'd been downstairs talking to Sean and felt it went well. Then I got up to go talk to him. Becky softly pleaded, "Be kind. Please be kind." It's sad that she even had to tell me that. After all, this was my son that I deeply loved.

I held in my heart her gentle plea as I went downstairs to Sean's room. His door was shut, and as I knocked softly, I was still trying to find the right words to say. When my son opened the door, all I could do was give him a big hug and say, "I love you." (Years later, Sean told me that it was exactly what he needed to hear, and those words, along with the hug, meant the world to him.)

As we sat down on his bed, Sean told me how hard it had been for him over the years. "Dad, you know you've said some really mean things." He was right. In my mind, I had figured that gay people had chosen their lifestyle, and if they'd chosen it, then they deserved whatever negativity I expressed about them.

I didn't even know what to say in reply. The world around me had shifted, and I had no words to describe what I was feeling. All I could come up with was, "Hey, let's get some sleep and we'll talk about it later."

Soon Sean went back to college without hearing another word from me. That's when I decided I would try to "fix" him. I read everything I could about the topic from a "Church" perspective, and then I sent him what I'd learned. I naively assumed that Sean hadn't already read far more than I had concerning the topic. Still, he patiently read each letter and responded with something else written from his perspective. I couldn't understand why he didn't see things the same way I did.

I remained closed-minded far longer than I care to admit. I kept desperately hoping that his "gayness" would go away in time. I figured it was just a phase.

I spent the next couple of years still misunderstanding what my son was going through. When Sean returned home again for his Christmas break, I looked forward to our traditional father and son coyote hunting trip and thought he was looking forward to it too—including the four-hour trip there and back the same day. Sean and my youngest son, Skye, were the only ones who went with me that year. We had a good time together, even though we didn't shoot a single coyote, and I enjoyed spending time in the outdoors with family. Coyotes or not, I considered it a successful day.

On the way back, we talked about lots of things, except "it." I wasn't sure we should talk about it with Skye in the car. I think part of me felt that if we didn't talk about it, we could pretend everything was just fine with Sean and our relationship. Again, I was unaware of just how much I misunderstood what Sean was going through. I figured he was Mormon, after all. He was a returned missionary. He was such a good young man with a strong spirit, and I kept believing that he would soon "come back around." What good would talking about it really do? Ignoring it might be the way to go.

Sean knew better. On the drive home, he said, "Dad, I thought we were going to talk. I mean, really talk." There we were, stuck in the truck, so I had nowhere to run or hide. Then I made the ill-fated mistake of really letting him have it. I was his father, after all. I figured that's what I should do since I had stewardship over him. However, I unwittingly yielded unrighteous dominion as I came back at him.

"All right, let's talk about it," I said it with all the indignation I thought a "righteous father" should be showing. Forgetting, of course, important lessons from God, like that of the father of the prodigal son. Upon seeing his son "a great way off," without knowing whether or not his son wanted to live the life he'd taught him, he "had compassion, and ran, and fell on his neck, and kissed him." On the contrary, I was ready to attack my son. I went at him with both barrels, using all the ammunition I'd saved up for just such an occasion.

"Sean, why on earth would you choose such a thing? Why?"

He just looked at me and chuckled. It was not an in-your-face kind of laugh or a happy kind of laugh. It was just a chuckle filled with a certain resignation. He was hoping his own father would show more compassion and true Christlike love than he had been receiving from other Latter-day Saints. No doubt he had heard that question so many times that it seemed ridiculous. Instead of coming back at me with the same anger I'd just shown him, he responded with compassion and a deep sadness.

"Dad, I didn't choose this. Why would I choose to be part of a group of people who face more misunderstanding and judgment than nearly any other group, especially in the Church? Why would anyone choose this?"

That's when it finally hit me. I suddenly saw all the pain and suffering he'd endured from the jokes, stories, and comments about gays I'd made around him, not knowing he was gay. I thought I was justified and even funny. "Those gays" were not part of "my people." Plus, I saw myself as sort of a "man's man." I loved sports, fishing, and hunting—the great outdoors. I was homophobic without even realizing it as I said all those mean things while Sean was growing up. I didn't know he was dying inside, shrinking, as he thought, "My dad has no idea that he's talking about me."

All those times came flooding back to me, and I saw the pain my son had gone through alone, largely from my ignorant words and actions. That moment was such a powerful realization for me. An about-face. For the first time, I got a glimpse of what Sean had been through and what he must have been facing day after day, year after year.

Then, by the grace of God, inspiration came flooding in. My crusty exterior gave way to "a broken heart and a contrite spirit." I remembered a story I'd heard years before. A sportswriter was assigned to cover the Olympics—the rowing, canoeing, and kayaking. (It was about sports and the outdoors, so of course I paid attention.) He interviewed one of the team captains and asked, "What about the wind? What about the rain? What about the wake from the other boats?"

The team captain responded to each question with "that's outside my boat." When the journalist finally asked what he meant, the captain said, "I cannot control those things. It doesn't do me any good to worry about them. I focus on the things that are in my boat."

Talking with Sean, I realized I'd been trying to "fix" him, and that wasn't my job, nor was it what he needed. His being gay was not in my boat. It was in the Savior's boat. I realized I'd been judgmental and selfish. I'd forgotten that as Christians, we are to let Christ be the judge, and He is the only one who can be. None of us truly knows everything about anyone else's life, but the Savior knows.

In that moment, I chose to put it in Christ's boat where it belonged. What was left in my boat was the divine call to love my son. That was far more helpful and Christlike than the other stuff I'd been putting in there. It also served as an important reminder that all of my kids need my love—the love of an earthly father who seeks after divine qualities.

Even though my seemingly bright idea to try to fix Sean had come from a place of love, as far as I was concerned, Sean was feeling the opposite. My comments to him felt rejecting, judgmental, and, worst of all, like I didn't really love him for who he is—at any given moment and in all things.

I wondered why it had been so difficult for me to have Christlike love for others, especially my own son. I'd been stirring up contention rather than fostering feelings of love and a sense of belonging.

In the Book of Mormon, the Savior clearly warns about the dangers of contention. In what little time He had with the Nephites after His resurrection, He told them, "For verily, verily I say unto you, he that hath the spirit of contention is not of me, but is of the devil, who is the father of contention, and he stirreth up the hearts of men to contend with anger, one with another" (3 Nephi 11:29).

The Savior wasn't simply talking to those who may not have been keeping the commandments, or even those who were. He warned against contention expressed by *anyone*, especially those who are doing their best to obey the covenants made at baptism, whether we are dealing with our friends or those we might consider our enemies. The "father of contention" is the devil. The Savior is the Prince of Peace.

As I focused on what was in my boat—loving my son—the contention ceased. My unconditional love for my son was no longer a topic of debate; rather, it was a means of strengthening my family and becoming more like our Savior. Once I understood this, that's when our conversations became more frequent and meaningful. I let go of my need to "fix" Sean.

When Sean returned home for visits, we spent time together in positive ways and in open communication. The words "I love you" were no longer just words. Instead, I was finally able to demonstrate my sincere love for my son through my actions.

That was put to the test when we got the news that Sean was engaged to his boyfriend of two years. Sean told us the beautiful story of their engagement. Why wasn't I feeling the joy for him that I thought I'd be feeling? As other family members were cheering and hollering congratulations, why wasn't I?

My mind immediately went back to a moment only the week before when I spoke to a large group of parents. After my presentation, people surrounded me and bombarded me with questions. One woman in particular had learned of her daughter's coming out just six days prior to the event.

She said, "I'm not happy for her and the road she's going down with a partner. I don't like faking happy. Is that what I am supposed to do since you have told us to simply love our children and give them their agency that Heavenly Father gave us? How do I do that? It will seem so fake when my feelings aren't happy for her."

I remember thinking that it was important to emphasize that she love her daughter and try to be happy for her, even if she has to fake it for a time. I said that the journey we each take is different. As parents, we might try to take choice or agency away from our children. We don't want them to fail, feel pain, or know heartache. But life doesn't work that way. It can be through our failings that we learn our greatest lessons.

I then explained that her daughter may be experiencing great joy by feeling loved and validated in ways that she had not felt before. We spoke of the gift of having her daughter in her life instead of shutting her out by building walls between them.

I spoke of the hurdles we must all go over—even when we feel we have it all figured out and are doing exactly what the

Savior intended us to do. We might be running along just fine, and then—bam! Right in front of us, there's a hurdle.

Sure enough, just a week later—bam! Right in front of me. I'm hit with the news that my son is going to marry another man, and it seems all I can hear is "my son is marrying another man."

Then I heard my own voice reminding me that this is my son's journey of happiness. He is doing what he feels he needs to do in order to find the joy and happiness we all seek. As parents, isn't that what we want for our children, for them to be happy?

I knew I needed to be happy for Sean and that I could be happy for him. So I announced it to a few family members and friends. I answered excited questions and found myself feeling joy in his journey. I told them what a great person his fiancé is. I even joked and laughed as I told them that his fiancé is a returned missionary. I would tell them, "Isn't that every Mormon parent's dream, that their child will marry a returned missionary?"

I discovered, through my own experiences, that I really didn't have to fake happiness for him. I could feel genuinely happy.

I do enjoy my son-in-law and have felt love for him. I know that Heavenly Father loves him and wants him to return home, just as He does Sean.

It doesn't need to make perfect sense to me. I am learning that many things might not make sense, at least to my understanding. I have learned to celebrate the victories whenever and from wherever they come.

My son is in a loving, committed relationship. That is a victory.

He's married a person who had the courage and desire to serve his Heavenly Father and Savior for two years. That is a victory.

He did not have to struggle with drug or alcohol addiction to numb the pain of a rejecting family who might have kicked him out of the house (mistakenly thinking it would somehow help the situation). That is a victory.

I celebrate the victories with him, and know that I have a Savior who created a way to resolve even the things that don't make sense to me. I love and trust Him and his Atonement, and that is a victory.

Don't get me wrong. I still have my moments where the "old Scott" creeps in. I'm not always kind and charitable. But now I realize that personal reformation and true conversion begin with a change of heart. As I have recognized the need and felt the desire, I've prayed fervently for Heavenly Father to change my heart. Before that, I had been praying that God would "change" my son. Yet, all the while, it was my heart, might, mind, and soul that were in need of changing.

An old Protestant hymn comes to mind, one that I heard Sister Neill F. Marriott recite in a general conference talk:

Have Thine own way, Lord!
Have Thine own way!
Thou art the Potter;
I am the clay.
Mold me and make me
After Thy will,
While I am waiting,
Yielded and still.[47]

The change in my relationship with Sean didn't come about because I changed Sean or because God changed him. Rather, it came to pass because I realized that I was the one who needed to change, and the Lord has been helping me do so. He heard my prayers and patiently waited until I was ready to receive the true answers to my beseeching. In His infinite wisdom, He helped me

---

47. See Neill F. Marriott, "Yielding Our Hearts to God," *Ensign*, November 2015.

put aside my pride and let Him be the potter. I am the clay, or, at least, I try to be the clay as often as possible.

Some people think that because we love our gay son we must have distanced ourselves from the Church. Loving unconditionally doesn't mean leaving the Church because of what a child might be going through.

Other people think that we must not really love our son, because if we did, we wouldn't still be in the Church.

Becky and I have found that living the gospel is the best thing we can do for Sean and all our family. The core of the gospel is love: love for God, love for our fellowman, and love for ourselves. For us, turning our back on any family member would, in fact, be turning our back on the Savior. He tells us, "Inasmuch as ye have done it unto one of the least of these my brethren, ye have done it unto me" (Matthew 25:40).

One of the things I told Sean after he came out to us was that we would never turn our back on him or leave the Church for him or anyone else. We are grateful that he said he doesn't expect us to. We love our son, and we love the gospel. I'm so humbled and thankful to be married to a woman who believes the same things I do.

As Becky and I listen to our Church leaders during conferences, we're increasingly grateful this topic is being addressed. We often wish we'd had the benefit of hindsight when we were raising our children. I have no doubt that the Church's recent resources will continue to help us along this journey. Because each journey is different, I trust that the Lord will travel our unique road right alongside us, carrying us when necessary as He sees fit. His direct revelation has softened my heart.

To parents, especially you fathers who may be having a difficult time accepting your child, I would say, please turn to the Lord as best you can. Lay it all at His feet, and He will guide you along. He can soften hearts and bring families closer. Children need parents, and if we respond in love, it can make all the difference in the world.

ABOUT THE AUTHORS

Becky Mackintosh is a popular speaker known for her inspirational stories, honest approach, and open heart. She is dedicated to her family and her faith as a member of The Church of Jesus Christ of Latter-day Saints. Her love for humanitarian work inspired her to volunteer in India and Africa, which is a reflection of the selfless service she renders within the walls of her own home. She is the proud and humbled mother of seven children and an ever-growing number of grandchildren. She lives in Lehi, Utah, with her husband, Scott, in a nest that's never quite empty.

Scott Mackintosh grew up in Salt Lake City. He has the gift of making friends with everyone he meets. Scott served a two-year mission for The Church of Jesus Christ of Latter-day Saints to Scotland (the land of his ancestry). He has a diverse background in sales and construction. His happy place is in the mountains. His scripture hero is Enos for his great faith and his ability to hunt with a bow (another of Scott's passions). Scott and his wife, Becky, are the parents of seven children.

Sean Mackintosh is the third child of seven. At the age of twenty-four, he came out to his parents as gay. He served a two-year mission for The Church of Jesus Christ of Latter-day Saints to the Michigan Detroit Mission. He graduated with his bachelor's in social work from Brigham Young University–Hawaii and received his master's degree in social work mental health from the University of Hawaii. He raises French Bulldogs and is a proud bee keeper. He and his husband reside in Utah.